GRAVE MATTERS

GRAVE MATTERS

Compiled by E. R. Shushan

A CURIOUS COLLECTION
OF 500 ACTUAL EPITAPHS,
FROM WHICH WE LEARN
OF GRIEVING SPOUSES,
FATAL GLUTTONY,
VENGEFUL RELATIONS, AND
ALL MANNER OF
PARTING COMMENTARY

BALLANTINE BOOKS · NEW YORK

Library of Congress Catalog Card Number: 89-92596

ISBN: 0-345-36470-8

Text design by Holly Johnson
Cover design by James R. Harris
Cover photography copyright © 1989 by Frederic L. Dodnick

Manufactured in the United States of America

First Edition: October 1990
10 9 8 7 6 5 4 3 2 1

Contents

•

Introduction

•

The quest for immortality has obsessed humanity since the beginning of time. Epitaphs have in many ways served to quench this desire. They are a continuing dialogue between the dead and the living, providing histories, warnings, prayers, and comfort to those who come after.

The Ancient Egyptians succeeded in this quest like no other civilization. The building of the tombs and pyramids and the preservation of the bodies achieved two purposes: they recorded the history of the deceased, and reminded the living of their own mortality. The Greeks did not consider the identification of the deceased essential. Their epitaphs, written in verse, reminded the reader of the universality of death. One, composed by Plato, refers to two tombs that were next to each other:

> This is a sailor's—that a ploughman's tomb;
> thus sea and land abide one common doom.

The Romans buried their dead alongside major highways, so that they might be a constant reminder to the living. Unlike the Greeks, they immortalized their dead with a portrait and an inscription which included the person's name, his position, and the names of the relatives who buried him.

Epitaphs—in fact, all identified graves—disappeared along with the great ancient civilizations and did not appear again until the eleventh century, the only exceptions being for royalty, clergy, and saints. At this time, the most consistent theme in epitaphs made its reappearance: *Memento mori*, "remember you must die," a direct address from the dead to the living. It was already a prevailing theme by 1376, when Edward the Black Prince was buried in Canterbury Cathedral. His epitaph, written in French, reads in part:

> Whoe'er thou art with lips comprest,
> That passest where this corpse doth rest,
> To that I tell thee, list, O man!
> So far as I to tell thee can,
> Such as thou art, I was but now
> And as I am so shalt be thou.

Through the nineteenth century, versions of that idea—the dead speaking to a stranger and warning him of his fate—are the most prevalent of epitaphs:

> Stranger, stop and cast an eye,
> As you are now, so once was I.
> As I am now, so you will be,
> Prepare for death and follow me.

By the fifteenth century, epitaphs had largely taken on the form that would remain until the twentieth century, combining the name and dates of birth and death with biographical information, ensuring the immortality of the dead for at least as long as the life of the stone. King Richard III, who was killed in 1484, had his epitaph composed by the order of King Henry VII, who defeated him. This effectively secured history as Henry saw it, and propagated the story of the little princes and the wicked uncle which remained unquestioned for almost five hundred years.

Sir Thomas More, who wrote the first history of Richard III, following the somewhat specious lead of his king and patron, Henry VIII's father, found it necessary to protect his own posterity by composing his own epitaph. This was a common custom, particularly among famous people, in order to ensure that the record—as they knew it—be correct. More's, which runs several pages, is written in Latin and recounts not only his own history, but that of his father and his children.

This tradition carried forward for hundreds of years. By the eighteenth century, those believing themselves to be eligible for the Poet's Corner in Westminster Abbey conducted great debates about the function of epitaphs. Dr. Samuel Johnson felt that they should be "in honour of the person deceased." Taking his lead, eulogies for the illustrious and wellborn took on massive proportions as written by the great authors of the day, their primary concern being laudatory commentary rather than honest reflection. The practice continued well into the late nineteenth century.

The common folk of both England and America stumbled along as best they could with verse composed either by themselves or by the stonecutters, rendering their own histories in churchyards and burial grounds. But the desire was the same—to grasp a bit of immortality by having the last word and warning the living that everyone is equal in the end.

In the nineteenth century, mourning became something of an art, with the funeral as the center of the spectacle. Poor families did without necessities to be able to afford a decent funeral and headstone. Epitaphs were often chosen from books in stonecutters' offices, containing a verse for every situation and condition. Families, often including the about-to-be-deceased, pored over these books, looking for an epitaph that fit perfectly—in much the same way as we choose names for babies.

By the 1860s, a movement to reform the cemeteries had begun. Its proponents argued that headstones should be smaller and less expensive, and epitaphs should be shorter and less laudatory. The movement took hold by the beginning of the twentieth century, resulting in the still common practice of including only the name of the deceased, as well as dates of birth and death, on a modest stone marker.

In England, the gathering of epitaphs as chronicles of the past began too late to save what was lost during the suppression of the monasteries and the subsequent zeal of the Puritans. By the sixteenth century, this written record of the people was beginning to be recognized as a part of history that had been ignored. Queen Elizabeth I issued a proclamation in 1560 "against breaking or defacing Monuments of antiquitie . . ." In the early seventeenth century, the first collections of English epitaphs were printed; John Weever provided the first important work, *Ancient Funeral Monuments*, in 1619. John Le Neve published his massive five-volume opus, entitled *Monumenta Anglicana*, in 1719.

But as the ancient burial grounds crumbled and disappeared, and debate continued about the importance of recording actual names and places, much was lost. In addition, a new religious fervor emerged, and those epitaphs considered blasphemous were intentionally deleted from any record. A famous example that did not make it into the definitive work of the nineteenth century, Pettigrew's *Chronicles of the Tombs*, is:

> Here lye I
> Martin Elginbrodde
> Hae mercy o' my soul
> Lord God
> A' I wad do were I
> Lord God
> And ye were
> Martin Elginbrodde.

The idea that man should presume to tell God his business was inexcusable, and certainly the highest form of blasphemy.

By 1857 Pettigrew was questioning the validity of Weever's sources, and pushing for the establishment of a Public Register of Inscriptions. (Even in the early seventeenth century, Weever had to make do with fragments of inscriptions, and as the remaining headstones disintegrated as well, it was impossible to record with certainty what was originally written. With the loss of the monuments, even he had to trust his only sources.)

By the early nineteenth century, the graveyards of America were beginning to disappear. Churches made their own records in some cases; but the first burial grounds, which in Puritan times were not attached to churches, were forgotten.

In 1878 William Whitmore made a major study of the Boston area graveyards. He felt it was only important to record the names and dates, adding "followed by four lines of verse" after each entry to indicate that there had been an epitaph included. Modern chronicler Fritz Spiegl points out that "anthologists have been merrily anthologizing from each other for nearly two centuries." But, in fact, it is virtually the only way of preserving the wealth of information that has been recorded. Even the cemeteries of the nineteenth century are now falling into ruin, and their portion of human history along with them.

The progress of the American spirit can be chronicled by simply examining the epitaphs. Grim death was a part of everyday life for the early settlers. As times got easier, so did death; warnings of what was to come, along with the stories of what had been, were replaced by hopes of eternal peace, and finally by just a simple stone recording the dates someone had lived. The scarcity and cost of suitable stone forced many early Americans, especially those in the South and West, to use wood. Those pioneer markers had been completely lost before anyone thought to record their histories. The ones that remain, particularly from the old West, give us a picture of life exactly as we expect it to be.

In our society, the desire for actual immortality has been replaced to a great extent by the "technical" immortality of embalming and brass coffins. Ensuring loved ones eternal rest within the grave has become more important than guaranteeing them eternal fame above it. Table talk of epitaphs is considered morbid, and the witty parlor games of composing one's own have disappeared. These two famous episodes are reminders of the way the game used to be played:

In the 1680s, King Charles II of England and his favorite, the Earl of Rochester, composed epitaphs for each other.

Rochester said:

"Here lies our sovereign Lord, the King
    Whose word no man relied on;
He never said a foolish thing,
    Nor ever did a wise one."

Charles replied:

"If Death could speak, the King would say
    In justice to his crown:
His acts they were his ministers.
    His words they were his own."

In the twentieth century, gallows humor continued at the Algonquin Round Table. Dorothy Parker's epitaph for herself was "Excuse my dust." Franklin Pierce Adams said, "Pardon me for not rising," and George S. Kaufman composed, "I knew something like this would happen."

Now practically a lost art, epitaphs provide history, humor, and indeed, a measure of immortality for those who are remembered.

GRAVE MATTERS

Grieving Spouses

•

Divorce was not an option for centuries, primarily for religious reasons, so the pledge of "till death do you part" was a threat to be believed. Death emancipated the suffering, and they recorded their liberation on the tomb of the deceased.

It is interesting to note that a great many more men than women seemed pleased to be free of their marital vows. Women, on the whole, appeared more charitable, even in death.

To be fair, the language of the time can be misinterpreted, making a sincere statement of grief sound like joy. And, to be sure, there are quite a few who lived in bliss for many years. But, as a group, the surviving spouses are among the most prolific.

•

MATHIES BRANDEN

> Passing stranger, call it not,
> A place of fear and doom,
> I love to linger o'er this spot,
> It is my husband's tomb.

Bismarck, North Dakota
1882

MARY FORD

Here lies Mary, the wife of John Ford,
We hope her soul is gone to the Lord;
But if for Hell she has changed this life,
She had better be there than John Ford's wife.

Wiltshire, England
1790

●

RICHARD TULLY

Here lies old Mr. Richard Tully
Who lived an C and 3 years fully
And threescore years before the Mayor,
The sword of the city he did bear.
Nine of his wives do by him lie
So shall the tenth when she doth die.

Gloucester, England
1736

JOHN DALE

Know posterity that on the 8th of April in the
year of Grace 1757 the rambling remains of the
above said John Dale were in the 86th year of his
pilgrimage, laid upon his two wives.

This thing, in life might cause some jealousy:
Here all three lie together lovingly,
But from embraces here no pleasure flows,
Alike are here all human joys and woes.
Here Sarah's chiding John no longer hears,
And John's rambling Sarah no more fears:
A period's come to all their toilsome lives:
the Goodman's quiet, still are both of his wives.

Derby, England
1757

●

JOANNA WILDER

Joanna Wilder
born Mar. 10, 1765
died Dec. 15, 1845
Aged 80 years, 8 months & 5 days

She fulfilled in a good degree the
Scripture requirements for the wife
of a Decon.
She lived with her husband 60 years.

Dummerston, Vermont
1845

5

WILLIAM AND SARAH THOMPSON

In rememberance of
WILLIAM · THOMPSON
Who departed this life
Also SARAH, his wife,
Departed Oct 10th 1789, aged 78 years.
She was afterwards married to John Jackson,
Whose remains lie near this place.

Braithwell, England
1789

●

ELIZABETH HAMILTON

Here lies the body of
Elizabeth
wife of
Major General
Hamilton

Who was married forty seven years
and never did *one* thing
To disoblige her husband

London, England
1746

CHARLES WARD

In Memory of Charles Ward
who died May 1770
aged 63 years
A dutiful Son
A loving Brother
and
An affectionate Husband

This stone was not erected by
Susan his Wife. She erected a stone
to John Salter her second husband
forgetting the affection of Charles
Ward, her first Husband.

Lowestoft, England
1770

●

JARED BATES

Sacred to the Memory of Mr.
Jared Bates who Died Aug. the 6th
1800. His Widow aged 24 who mourns
as one who can be comforted lives
at 7 Elm Street this village
and possesses every qualification
for a good wife.

Lincoln, Maine
1800

MARTHA BLEWIT

Martha Blewit
of the
Swan, Baythorn-End
of this parish
Buried May 7th 1681
Was the wife of 9 Husbands
successively
but the 9th outlived her
The text to her Funeral
Sermon was
"Last of all the Woman
dyed alsoe"

Chelmsford, England
1681

●

JOHN AND AGNES DEN

On John and Agnes Den

Here lyes under this ston,
John Den barber-surgeon
And Agnes hys wyf, who to hevven went,
MC CCC and x that is verament,
For whos soul, of your charite,
Say a paternoster and an ave.

London, England
1410

MARY SMITH

Here lieth Mary, never was contrary
To me nor her neighbours around her.
Like Turtle and Dove we lived in love
And I left her where I may find her.

Orpington, England
1755

●

THE DUDLEY FAMILY

God be praised:
Here is Mr. **Dudley**, senior,
And **Jane** his wife also,
Who, while living was his superior,
But see what death can do.
Two of his sons also lie here,
One **Walter** t'other **Joe**.
The all of them went in the year
1510 below.

Broome, England
1510

SARAH HAYES

Here lies the Body
of
SARAH
wife of
JOHN HAYES
who died
24 March 1823 AD
aged 42 years

*The Lord giveth
And the Lord taketh away
Blessed be the name of the Lord*

*Fife, Scotland
1823*

•

LIDIA PALMER

In Memory of
Lidia ye Wife of
Mr. Simeon Palmer
who died Decem
ye 26 1754 in ye 35th
Year of her Age.

In Memory of
Elizabeth who
should have been the
Wife of Mr.
Simeon Palmer
who died Aug. 14th
1776 in the 64th Year
of her age.

*Little Compton, Rhode Island
1776*

WARREN GIBBS

Warren Gibbs
Died by arsenic poisoning
Mar. 23, 1860
Aged 36 yrs. 5 mo. 23 dys.

Think my friends when this you see
How my wife has done for me
She in some oysters did prepare
Some poison for my lot and fare
Then of the same I did partake
And Nature yielded to its fate
Before she my wife became
Mary Felton was her name.

Pelham, Massachusetts
1860

●

MARY MARTIN

Here lies the wife of Roger Martin
She was a good wife to Roger, that's sartin.

Ockham, England
c. 1800

11

PHILLIP AND ELLEN MAINWARING

Lyke as this marble now doeth hyde
the bodies of theisse twayne,
So shall not thou on earth lyve longe
but turne to dust agayne.
Then learne to dye and dye to lyve
as theisse two heare example give.

Over Peover, England
1573

•

ANNA WALLACE

The children of Israel wanted bread,
And the Lord he sent them manna,
Old Clerk Wallace wanted a wife,
And the Devil he sent him Anna.

Ribbesford, England
c. 1770

•

LURANA NICHOLS

Here lies the remains of H. P. Nichols' wife,
Who mourned away her natural life.
She mourned herself to death for her man,
While he was in the service of Uncle Sam.

Fletcher, Vermont
1863

MRS. EUNICE PAGE

Five times five years I lived a virgin's life
Nine times five years I lived a virtuous wife;
Wearied of this mortal life, I rest.

Plainfield, Vermont
1888

●

MARTHA WELLS

MARTHA WELLS, WIFE OF JOHN WELLS
Obiit 1777

We far from home did come
Each other for to join
In peace with all Men here we liv'd
And did in Love Combine
But oh remark the Strange
Yet heavn's wise decree
I'm lodg'd within the Silent grave
He's rouling in the Sea.

Orpington, England
1777

JOAN CARTHEW

Here lies the body of JOAN CARTHEW,
Born at St. Columb, died at St. Crew.
Children she had five,
Three are dead & two are alive.
Those that are dead choosing rather
To die with their mother, than live with their father.

Saint Crewe, England
c. 1780

●

WILLIAM SUNDERLAND AND HIS FIVE WIVES

Here lie the five wives of *William Sunderland*,
Also William Sunderland
1790

Haworth, England
1750

●

SUSAN PATISON

To free me from domestic strife
Death called at my house—but he spoke to my wife.
Susan, wife of David Patison lies here
Oct. the 19th 1706
Stop, Reader! and if not in a hurry, Shed a tear.

Hadleigh, England
1706

ANN HUGHES

Who far beneath this tomb doth rest,
Has joined the army of the blest.
The Lord had ta'en her to the sky:
The Saints rejoice—and so do I.

Cherening-le-Clay, England
c. 1750

●

ANONYMOUS

Here lies my wife
Here lies she,
Hallelujah!
Hallelujee!

Ulverston, England
c. 1750

●

JEMMY LITTLE

Here lies JEMMY · LITTLE, a carpenter industrious
A very good-natured man, but somewhat blusterous.
When that his little wife his authority withstood,
He took a little stick & banged her as he would.
His wife now left alone, her loss does so deplore,
For now he's dead & gone this fault appears so small
A little thing would make her think it is no fault at all.

Portsmouth, England
c. 1750

15

SETH J. MILLER

My wife from me departed
And robbed me like a knave
Which caused me broken hearted
to descent into my grave.
My children took an active part
And to doom me did contrive,
Which struck a dagger to my heart
Which I could not survive.

Rehoboth, Maine
1848

●

JOSEPH SEWELL

Here lies the body of Joe Sewell,
Who to his wife was very cruel
And likewise to his brother Tom,
As any man in Christendom.
This is all I'll say of Joe,
There he lies and let him go.

Great Cornard, England
c. 1800

RICHARD AND MARY PRITCHARD

Here lies the man RICHARD,
And MARY his wife;
Their surname was PRITCHARD
They lived without strife.
And the reason is plain:
They abounded in riches,
They had no care of pain,
And—the wife wore the breeches.

Essex, England
c. 1690

●

CHARITY BLIGH

CHARITY, wife of GIDEON BLIGH
Underneath this stone doth lie
Naught was she e'er known to do
That her husband told her to.

Devonshire, England
c. 1650

PATIENCE JOHNSON

PATIENCE
wife of Shadrack Johnson
Shadrack! Shadrack!
The Lord grant unto thee
PATIENCE
Who *laboured* long and *patiently*
In her vocation;
But her patience being exhausted
She departed in the midst of her *labour*
AEt 38
May she rest from her *labours*
The mother of 24 children & died in childbed,
June 6, 1717 Aged 38 years.

Bedford, England
1717

●

ROBERT LODER

I would have all my neighbors be all kind and mild,
Quiet and civil to my dear wife and child.

Marston, England
1768

RICHARD AND SUSAN SCARCHERD

That Dick loved Sue was very true;
Perhaps you'll say What's that to you?

That she loved Dick, & in its this:
That Dick loved Sue, & that made bliss.

South Cave, England
c. 1850

●

FRANCIS AND MARY HUNTRODDS

Here lies the bodies
of FRANCIS HUNTRODDS & MARY his wife
Who were both born on the same day
of the week, month & year (viz) Sept ye
19th 1600, marry'd on the day of their
birth & after having had 12 children
born to them, died aged 80 years, on
the same day of the year they were born,
Sept 19th 1680 the one not above 5 hours before ye
other.

Husband & Wife that did twelve children bere
Dy'd the same day; alike both aged were,
Bout eighty years they liv'd, five hours did part
(Even on the marriage day) each tender heart
So fit a match, surely could never be
Both in their lives & their death agree.

Whitby, England
1680

JACOB JONES

The body underneath this stone is
Of my late husband, Jacob Jones,
Who, when alive, was an Adonis
    Ah! well-a-day!
O Death! thou spoiler of fair faces
Why took'st thou him from my embraces?
How could'st thou mar so many graces?
    Say, tyrant, say.

Swansea, Wales
c. 1700

•

ANTHONY DRAKE

Sacred to the memory of ANTHONY DRAKE
Who died for peace & quietness sake;
His wife was constantly scolding & scoffin'
So he sought for repose in a twelve-dollar coffin.

Burlington, Massachusetts
c. 1800

JOHN MacQUEELIN

> Here on the grave of John
> MacQueelin,
> I, his wife, am humbly kneelin'
> If John was alive and had his
> feelin'
> I would be dead and he would be
> kneelin'.

Londonderry, Ireland
c. 1775

●

ALICE CUTT

> Two happy days assigned me to men,
> Of wedlock and of death! O happy then!
> 'Mongst women was she that is here interr'd
> Who live'd out two and dying had the third.

Iver, England
1634

●

THOMAS ALLEYN AND HIS TWO WIVES

THOMAS ALLEYN AND HIS TWO WIVES
> Death here advantage hath of life I spye,
> One husband with two wifes at once may lye.

Witchingham, England
1650

"IN MEMORIAM"

In Memoriam
I plant these shrubs upon your grave, dear wife,
That something on this spot may boast of life.
Shrubs must wither and all earth must rot!
Shrubs may revive: but you, thank heaven, will not.

Raydonshire, England
c. 1800

●

ANONYMOUS

This spot is the sweetest I've seen in my life,
For it raises my flowers and covers my wife.

[graveyard unknown] England
c. 1850

●

JOAN LEY

JOAN LEY
Here she Leys all mold in the grave
I Trust in God her Soul to save
And with her Saviour Christ to dwell
And there I home to Live as well.
This Composed by her Grateful Husband
NICHOLAS LEY 1759

Devon, England
1759

JOHN AND MARY COLLIER

> Here lies John & with him Mary
> Cheek by Jowl they never vary
>
> No wonder they so well agree
> John wants no punch & Moll no tea.

Rochdale, England
1786

•   •

THOMAS GARDINER

> Thomas Gardiner
> Historian of Southwald and Denwich, buried
> with his two wives, Honor and Virtue
>
> Between Honor and Virtue, here doth lie
> The remains of Old Antiquity

Southwald, England
c. 1750

THOMAS AND MARY BOND

Here lie the bodies
of THOMAS BOND and MARY his wife
She was temperate, chaste, and charitable;
BUT
She was proud, peevish, and passionate.
She was an affectionate wife, and a tender mother:
BUT
Her husband and child, whom she loved,
Seldom saw her countenance without a disgusting
frown,
Whilst she received visitors, whom she despised, with
an endearing smile.
Her behavior was discreet towards strangers;
BUT
Independent in her family.
Abroad, her conduct was influenced by good breeding;
BUT
At home, by ill temper.
She was a professed enemy to flattery,
And was seldom known to praise or commend;
BUT
The talents in which she principally excelled,
Were difference of opinion, and discovering flaws and
imperfections.
She was an admirable economist,
And without prodigality,
Dispensed plenty to every person in her family.
BUT
Would sacrifice their eyes to a farthing candle.
She sometimes made her husband happy with her good
qualities;

Much more frequently miserable—with her many
failings:
Insomuch that in thirty years cohabitation he often
lamented
That maugre all her virtues,
He had not, in the whole, enjoyed two years of
matrimonial comfort.

AT LENGTH

Finding that she had lost the affections of her husband,
As well as the regard of her neighbours,
Family disputes having been divulged by servants,
She died of vexation, July 20, 1768,
Aged 48 years.
Her worn out husband survived her four months and
two days,
And departed this life, Nov. 28, 1768,
In the 54th year of his age.

WILLIAM BOND, brother to the deceased, erected this
stone,
As a *weekly monitor*, to the surviving wives of this
parish,
That they may avoid the infamy
Of having their memories handed to posterity
With a PATCH WORK character.

Horsley-Down, England
1768

What's In A Name?

•

As if it weren't bad enough growing up with a funny name, many people went to their graves with jokes about their names engraved on their stones.

Punning epitaphs using the name of the deceased were common even in Greek and Latin inscriptions. The first appeared in English in the fifteenth century, and by the early seventeenth century were very widely used, even if in many cases they were unsuitable to the gravity of the situation.

Anagrams and acrostics using the name of the deceased were also popular, especially during the last half of the seventeenth century. It was believed to be a sure sign of real education, and naive poets stretched the point, but somehow managed to make it.

•

CAPTAIN THOMAS STONE

> As the Earth the Earth doth Cover
> So under this *Stone* lies another.

> > *Rotherhithe, England*
> > *1666*

DANIEL EVANCE

[Anagram:] I can deal even.
Who is sufficient for this thinge
Wifely to harpe on every string.
Rightly divide the word of truth
To babes and men, to age & youth?
One of a thousand—where's he found
Soe learned, pious, & profound?
Earth has but few—there is in heaven
One who answers—"I can deal even."

Isle of Wight, England
1652

●

ELIZABETH WOOD

Eliza's soul, a graft divine
With clay was fastened unto wood!
The tree did suddenly decline
The fruit was blasted in the bud.
The clay which Death broke off lies here, the wife
Is now engrafted on the Tree of Life.
Reader, expect not long to hold thy breath,
For heart of oak thou seest cut off by Death.

Devon, England
1662

Beneath this cold stone
Lies a son of the Earth;
His story is short,
Though we date from his birth;
His mind was as gross
As his body was big;
He drank like a fish,
And he ate like a pig.
No cares of religion,
Of wedlock, or state,
Did e'er, for a moment,
Encumber John's pate:
He sat, or he walk'd
But his walk was creeping,
Without foe, without friend,
Unnotic'd he died;
Not a single soul laugh'd
Not a single soul cried.
Like his four-footed namesake,
He dearly lov'd earth,
So the sexton has cover'd
His body with turf.

Worcester, England
1756

JOHN STARRE

John Starre
Starr on high!
Where should a starr be
But on high?
Tho' underneath
He now doth lie
Sleeping in the Dust
Yet shall he rise
More glorious than
The Starres in skies.

Devon, England
1633

●

THOMAS GREENHILL

Here once a Hill was fresh & Greene,
Now wither'd is not to be seene,
Earth to earth shovel's up is shut,
A Hill into a Hole is put.

Beddington, England
1634

ROGER EARTH

From Earth we came, to earth we must return
Witness this Earth that lies within this Urn.
Begot by Earth: born also of Earth's womb,
74 years lived Earth, now earth's his tomb
In earth Earth's body lies under this stone
But from this earth to Heaven Earth's soul is gone.

Dinton, England
1634

●

THOMAS MILES

This Tombstone is a *Milestone*—Hah! how so?
Beneath lies *Miles*—who's *Miles* below.
A little man he was, a dwarf in size,
But now stretch'd out, at least *Miles* long he lies;
His grave, tho' small, contains a space so wide,
'T has *Miles* in length, and *Miles* in bredth and
Miles in room beside.

London, England
1782

THOMAS MORE

Here lyes one *More*
& no more than he
One more & no more—
how can that be?
One *More* & no more
may well lye here alone
But here lyes one more
& that is more than one.

London, England
1670

●

THEOPHILUS CAVE

Here in this grave there lies one Cave:
We call a cave a grave.
If cave be grave, and grave be cave
Then reader judge I crave
Whether both Cave be in this grave
or grave lie here on Cave;
If grave in cave here would lie
then grave, where is thy victory?

Barrow-on-Stour, England
1564

ROBERT LONGE

The life of man is a true lottery,
Where venturous death draws forth lots short and
long:
Yet free from fraud and partial flattery
He shuffled shields of several size among,
Drew *Longe*; and so drew longer his short days
Th' Ancient of days beyond all time to praise.

Broughton-Gifford, England
1620

●

KATHERINE RANDALL

K ind reader judge, here's underlain
A hopeful, young, and virtuous maid,
T hrown from the top of earthly pleasure
H eadlong, by which she gain'd a treasure
E nvironed with heaven's power,
R ounded with angels for that hour
I n which she fell: God took her home
N ot by just law, but martyrdom.
E ach groan she fetch'd upon her bed
R oared out alout I'm Murdered
A nd shall this blood, which here doth lie
N vain for right and vengence cry?
D o men not think, tho' gone from hence,
A venge God can't his innocence?
L et bad men think, so learn ye good
L ive each that's here doth cry for blood.

Devon, England
1648

JOHN ROSEWELL

This grave's a bed of Roses
here doth ly
John Rosewell, Gent.
his wife, nine children by

Inglishcombe, England
1687

●

THOMAS COLE

Reader you have within this grave
a *Cole* raked up in dust:
His courteous fate saw it was late
And that to bed he must:
So all was swept up to be kept
Alive until the day
The trump should blow it up and show
The *Cole* but sleeping lay.

Then do not doubt, the *Cole's* not out,
Though it in ashes lies:

That little spark now in the dark
Will like a Phoenix rise.

Lillington, England
1669

BEZA. WOOD

In Memory of
Beza. Wood
Departed this life
Nov. 2, 1837
aged 45 yrs.

Here lies one Wood
Enclosed in wood
One Wood
Within another.
The outer wood
Is very good:
We cannot praise
The other.

Winslow, Maine
1837

●

SOLOMON PEASE

Under the sod and under the trees
Lies the body of Solomon Pease.
He is not here, there's only the pod:
Pease shelled out and went to God.

Barre, Vermont
1880

ROGER GARDINER

ROGER GARDINER
Who died April 13 1658 aged 21 years 9 months

Roger lies here before his hour
Thus does the Gardiner lose his flower.

Thunderbridge, England
1658

●

MRS. PENNY

Reader, if cash thou are in want of any
Dig five-feet deep, & you will find a *Penny.*

[graveyard unknown] England
c. 1750

●

PETER STILLER

As *still* as death poor *Peter* lies
And *Stiller* when alive was he
Still not without hope to rise
Though *Stiller* than he *still* will be.

London, England
1750

GRACE STEVENS

What tho' enclosed in silent celle,
Grace for a space with worms may dwell,
This truth we find in sacred story,
Death cannot long keep Grace from Glory.

Atherton, England
1652

•

JOHN BROOKE

J ohn Brooke of the Parish of Ashe
O nly he is now gone.
H is days are past, His corps is lay'd
N ow under this marble stone.

B rook strete he was the honour of
R ob'd now it is of name,
O nly because he had no sede
O r children to have the same;
K nowing that all must pass away,
E ven when God will, non can denay.

He passed in the year of Grace
One thusand fyve hundreth ffower scor & two it was
The sixteenthe daye of January, I tell now playne,
The five and twentieth yere of Elizabeth rayne.

Ash, England
1582

JOHN POTTER, D.D.

> Alack and well aday!
> *Potter* himself is turned to clay.

Canterbury, England
1747

●

BISHOP KITCHYNE

> If *Kitchyne* was his name, as I have found,
> The Death now keeps his Kitchyne underground;
> And hungry worms, that late of flesh do eat
> Their Kitchyne now devours instead of meat.

Saint Alsaph, Wales
c. 1650

●

SIR RICHARD WORME

> Does worm eat Worme? Knight Worme this truth
> confirms
> For here, with worms, lies Worme, a dish for worms.
> Does worm eat Worme? Sure Worme will this deny,
> For Worme with worms, a dish for worms don't lie
> 'Tis so, and 'tis not so, for free from worms
> 'Tis certain Worme is blest without his worms.

Peterborough, England
1589

MRS. ROSE SPARKE

Sixty eight years a fragrant rose she lasted,
Noe vile reproach her virtures ever blasted;
Her autume past expects a glorious springe,
A second better life more flourishing.
"Hearken unto me, ye holy children, and bud forth as
a Rose"

Bletchly, England
1615

●

JOHN SULLEN

Here lies *John Sullen*, and its God's will
He that was *Sullen* should be sullen still;
He still is sullen, if the truth ye see;
Knock until doomsday, *Sullen* will not speak.

[graveyard unknown] England
c. 1700

●

JONATHAN FIDDLE

Here lies the body of Jonathan Fiddle
In 1868, on the 30th day of June
He went out of tune.

[graveyard unknown] New Jersey
1868

Occupational Hazards

•

Nothing illustrated how a man lived his life better than his professional status. His occupation was often the object of jokes or puns as well as admiration. Epitaphs abound comparing the deceased's employment to that of the grim reaper. Even the respected and secure profession of clockmaker was subject to this treatment—no one could be sure he would not be the object of a joke after death.

•

THOMAS GOLDSMITH, PIRATE

Men that are virtuous serve the Lord:
And the devil's by his friends adored:
And as they merit get a place
Amidst the blest of hellish race.
Pray then ye learned clergy, show
Where can this brute, Tom Goldsmith, go?
Whose live was one continued evil,
Striving to cheat God, man and devil.

Dartmouth, England
1714

JOSEPH W. HOLDEN, ASTRONOMER

Prof. Holden
the old Astronomer
discovered that the Earth
is flat and stationary
and the sun and moon
do move.

East Otisfield, Maine
1900

●

JOHN SPONG, CARPENTER

Who many a sturdy oak had laid along,
Fell'd by Death's surer hatchet, here lies Spong.
Post oft he made yet ne'er a place could get,
And liv'd by railing, thou' he was no wit.
Old saws he had, altho' no antiquarian,
And styles corrected, yet no grammarian.
Long liv'd he Ockham's prime architect:
And lasting as his fame a tomb t'erect.
In vain we see an artist such as he
Whose pales and gates are for eternity.

Ockham, England
1736

JOHN BILBE, CLOCKMAKER

Bilbe, thy
Movements kept in play
For thirty years and more we say,
Thy Balance or thy
Mainspring's broke
And all thy movements cease to work.

Axbridge, England
1767

●

HUGH MORGAN, APOTHECARY

HUGH MORGAN
Sleepeth Here In Peace:
Whom men did late admire
For worthful Parts.
To Queen Elizabeth
He was chief 'pothecary
Till her Death

And in his science as he did excell
In her high favour he always did dwell
To God religious, to all men kind
Frank to the poor, rich in content of mind
These were his virtues, in these died he
When he had liv'd an 100 years and 3.

Battersea, England
1613

JOSEPH JORDON, AUCTIONEER

Fair Virtue's up old Time's the Auctioneer
A lot so lovely can't be bought too dear,
Be quick in your biddings ere you are too late,
Time will not dwell, the hammer will not wait.

Alton, England
1814

•

PHOEBE CREWE, MIDWIFE

In memory of Mrs. Phoebe Crewe
Who died May 28, 1817 aged 77 years.
Who, during forty years
Practice as a midwife
in this City, brought into
the world nine thousand
seven hundred and
thirty children.

Norwich, England
1817

BRYAN TUNSTALL, ANGLER

Here lies
Poor but Honest
Bryan Tunstall
He was a most expert
angler
Until *Death*, envious of
his mark
Threw out his line,
hooked him
and
Landed him here
the 21st day of April,
1790

Ripon, England
1790

●

FRANK ROW, GRAVESTONE CUTTER

Here lies the body of poor Frank Row,
Parish Clerk & Gravestone Cutter,
And this is writ to let you know,
What Frank for others used to do
Is now done for Frank by another.

Selby, England
1706

BENJAMIN LINTON, BLACKSMITH

His sledge and hammer
lie reclin'd
His bellows too have
lost their wind
His fire's extinct
his forge decayed
His vice all in the dust is
laid
His coal is spent
his iron gone
His last nail's driven
his work is done.

Blean, England
1842

●

ROBERT LIVES, LAWYER

Robert Lives Esq
a Barrister
So great a lover of peace
that when a contention arose
between LIFE & DEATH
he immediately yielded up
the GHOST
to end the dispute.
August 12 1819

Richmond, England
1819

OSWALD GARDNER, ENGINEER

My *Engine* now is cold and still
No water does my *boiler* fill
My *coke* affords its flame no more
My days of usefulness are o'er
My *wheels* deny their noted speed
No more my guiding hand they heed
My *whistle*, too, has lost its tone
Its shrill and thrilling sounds are gone
My *valves* are now thrown open wide
My *flangs* all refuse to guide
My *clacks* also though once so strong
Refuse their aid in the busy throng
No more I fell each urging breath
My *steam* is now condens'd in death

Life's *railway's* o'er, each *station's* past
In death I'm stopp'd and rest at last
Farewell, dear friends, and cease to weep
In CHRIST I'm SAFE, in HIM I sleep.

Cumberland, England
1840

●

REVEREND BEZALEEL PINNEO

During his ministry
He enjoyed 7 revivals,
Admitted 716 members,
Baptized 1,117 and
Buried 1,126 of his flock.

Milford, Connecticut
1849

BENJAMIN MASSIAH, CIRCUMCISER

Underneath this Tomb
lies interred
The Earthly Remains of
BENJAMIN MASSIAH
Late Merchant of this Island
who was universally
Beloved and Respected by
All that knew him and whose
Death
was much lamented.
He had been Reader of the
JEWS SYNAGOGUE
for many years without Fee or Reward
and performed the Office of
CIRCUMCISER
with Great Applause
and Dexterity.
He departed this life
on the 29 Adar 5542
Corresponding to
the 15th of March
1782
Aged 67 Years and Eight Months

Bridgetown, Barbados
1782

JOHN HALL, GROCER

Here lie the remains of
JOHN HALL, *grocer*
The world is not worth a *fig*, & I have good *raisons*
for saying so.

Dunmore, Ireland
1790

●

MRS. ANN CLARK, MIDWIFE

On helpless babes I did attend
Whilst I on earth my life did spend:
To help the helpless in their need
I was ready with care and speed.
Many from pain my hands did free
But none from death could rescu me
My course is run and hour is passed
And you is coming also fast.

John Bradley was the first child she received
Into this world in 1698, and since, above 5,000!

Tiverton, England
1733

JOHN ARCHER, SEXTON

Beneath this stone lies ARCHER JOHN,
Late Sexton I aver,
Who without tears for 34 years
Did carcases inter.
Till to his dismay, on a summer day,
Death to him once did say—
"Leave off your trade, Be not afraid
But follow me away."
Without reply, or word, or sigh,
The summons he obey'd
In seventeen hundred & sixty eight
Resigned his life & spade.

Selby, England
1768

MICHAEL TURNER, CHOIRMASTER

His duty done, beneath this stone
Old Michael lies at rest,
His rustic rig, his song, his jig,
Were ever of the best.

With nodding head the choir he led
That none should start too soon;
The second too, he sang full true,
The viol played the tune.

And when at last his age had passed,
One hundred less eleven,
With faithful cling to fiddle string
He sang himself to Heaven.

Warnham, England
1880

●

WILLIAM SCRIVENOR, COOK

Alas! Alas! WILL SCRIVENOR's dead, who by his art
Could make Death's Skeleton edible in each part.
Mourn, squeamish Stomaches, and ye curious Palates,
You've lost your dainty Dishes & your Salades;
Mourn for yourselves, but not for him i' the least,
He's gone to taste of a more Heav'nly Feast.

King's Lynn, England
1684

LUKE STURLEY, GRAVE DIGGER

The graves around for many a year
Were dug by him who slumbers here,
Till, worn with age, he dropped his spade,
And in the dust his bones are laid;
As he now mouldering shares the doom
Of those he buried in the tomb,
So will his body too with theirs arise
To share the judgements of the skies.

Kenilworth, England
1643

●

GEORGE FORDHAM, JOCKEY

Died Oct 12, 1887 in his 51st year.
"Tis the pace that kills."

Slough, England
1887

●

A. A. H., ARCHITECT

Thy mortal tenement, immortal germ,
Hath sunk to dust, while all thy words stand firm.
O may'st thou at the rising of the just
Thyself stand firm when all thy words are dust.

Liverpool, England
1858

HENRY CLEMENTSHAW, ORGANIST

In memory of

HENRY CLEMENTSHAW

Upwards of 50 years organist of this church,
who died May 7, 1821, aged 68

Now like an organ, robb'd of pipes and breath,
Its keys and stops are useless made by death,
Tho' mute & motionless in ruins laid,
Yet when rebuilt by more than mortal aid,
This instrument new voiced and tuned, shall raise,
, To God, its builder, hymns of endless praise.

Wakefield, England
1821

●

JOHN BILBIE, CLOCKMAKER

Bilbie, thy
Movements kept in play
For thirty years or more
We say.

Thy Balance or thy
Mainspring's broken
And all thy movements
(Cease to work).
John Bilbie, of this parish, Clockmaker, who died
Sept 13th 1767, aged 33 years.

Axbridge, England
1767

JONATHAN SOUTHWARD, BUTCHER

By these Inscriptions be it understood,
My occupation was in shedding blood,
And many a beast by me was weekly slain,
Hunger to ease & Mortals to maintain.
Now here I rests from Sin & Sorrow free,
By means of Him who shed his blood for me.

Colerne, England
1847

●

JANE PARKER, MIDWIFE

Here lyeth a midwife, brought to be
Deliveresse delivered;
Her body being churched here
Here soul give thanks in yonder spere.

Peterborough, England
1653

WILLIAM SMITH, BLACKSMITH

My Sledging hammer has declined
My Bellows too have lost their Wind
My Fire's extinct, My Forge decayed

My Coals are spent, My Iron's gone
My Nails are drove, My Work is done.

Bilton, England
1748

•

THOMAS TURAR, BAKER

Like to a Baker's Oven is the grave
Wherein the bodyes of the faithful have
A Setting in, and where they do remain
In hopes to Rise, and to be Drawn again;
Blessed are they who in the LORD are dead,
Though set like dough, they shall be Drawn like
Bread.

Brixton, England
1643

DAVID WALL, MUSICIAN

To the memory of
DAVID WALL
whose superior performance on the bassoon endeared
him to an extensive musical acquaintance.
His social life closed on the 4th Dec., 1796
In his 57th year.

Ashover, England
1796

●

SALVINO ARMOLO D'ARMATI, OPTICIAN

Here lies Salvino Armolo d'Armati
of Florence
the inventor of spectacles.
May God pardon his sins!
The year 1318

Florence, Italy
1318

●

"HATTER COX," HATTER

Nearby these grayrocks
Enclosed in a box
Lies Hatter Cox
Who died of Smallpox.

Boston, Massachusetts
1832

Leave Me Alone

•

As Shakespeare said in his epitaph: "Blessed be he that spares these stones, And curst be he that moves my bones." Many people were concerned about being disturbed after death, and others never liked having people around much anyway, even when they were alive. Still, the desire to have the last word was strong enough to cause the following grumps to grouse from the grave.

•

WILLIAM ASH

Reader, pass on, nor waste your precious time
On bad biography and murdered rhyme:
What I was before's well known to my neighbors
What I am now is no concern of yours.

Devon, England
1797

GEORGE WARMINGTON

Tis my request
My bones may rest
Within this chest
Without molest.

Cornwall, England
1727

•

R. PEACOCK

My good lads do not sit on this stone on
account you do disfigure it with your heels;
lean on it if you please.
Your, &c., R. Peacock

North Curry, England
c. 1840

ROBERT CRYTOFT

"Myself"

As I walked by myself, I talked to myself,
And thus myself said to me,
Look for thyself and take care of thyself
For nobody cares for thee.
So I turn'd to myself, and I answered myself
In the self-same reverie
Look to myself or look not to myself
the self-same thing will it be.

Hammerfield, England
1810

●

WILL WHEATLY

Whoever treadeth on this stone
I pray you tread most neatly
For underneath this same do lie
Your honest friend—
WILL WHEATLY
Ob. November 10 1683

London, England
1683

JAMES WELLS

Weep not for me, your tears are in vain
   (The term of my probation's o'er)
From me the tears can wash no stain.
   Weep for yourselves and sin no more.

Wigborough Green, England
1830

●

JEAN ANDERSON

Praises on tombs are vainly spent:
   A good name is a monument.

Hammersmith, England
1770

●

THOMAS WRIGHT

Farewell, vain world! I've had enough of thee;
   I value not what thou canst say of me;
Thy smiles I value not, nor frowns don't fear;
   All's one to me, my head is quiet here.
What faults you've seen in me, take care to shun,
Go home, and see there's something to be done.

London, England
1776

ANONYMOUS

My name, my country, what are they to thee?
What, whether high or low my pedigree?
Perhaps I far surpassed all other men;
Perhaps I fell below them all—what then?
Suffice it, stranger, that thou seest a tomb;
Thou knowst its use: it hides—no matter whom.

Cheraw, South Carolina
c. 1880

●

NAMELESS LADY

Doomes to receive half my soul held dear;
The other half with grief she left me here.
Ask not her name for she was true & just;
Once a fine woman, now a heep of dust.

Barton, England
1777

●

JOHN FULLER

Now I am dead and lyd in grave
And that my bones are rotten,
By this shall I remember'd be
Or else I am forgotten.

Uckfield, England
1610

CHARLES ROGERS

Passenger,
Spare to obliterate the name of
CHARLES ROGERS
whose body is here deposited,
unless you are convinced that he hath
injured you by word or deed.

Lawrence Poutney, England
1784

•

MICAH HALL

QUID ERAM, NESCITIS:
QUID SUM, SESCITIS:
UBI ABII, NESCITIS
VALETE.

(What I was you know not—
What I am you know not—
Whither I am gone you know not—
Go about your business.)

Castleton, England
1804

Old
Maids

•

In a time when marriages were made early and lasted forever, life centered around the family. Living as a single person, especially by choice, was extremely suspect. Widowed grandparents were taken in by younger family members and treated as wise elders. But what about that maiden aunt, who lived alone in her parents' house?

If the following inscriptions are to be believed, to live and die unmarried was quite an embarrassment. "Eccentric" became the adjective that automatically preceded "maiden." It may be hard to accept that living life alone was their most memorable quality, but nevertheless, these unfortunate people were all victims of their heirs' "last laugh."

MARTHA DIAS

Here lyeth ye body of
MARTHA DIAS
always noisy not very pious
Who live to ye age of
3 score and 10
And gave to worms
What she refus'd to men.

Shropshire, England
c. 1675

●

MARGARET ROBINSON

This maid no elegance of form possessed;
No earthly love defil'd her sacred breast;
Hence free she liv'd from the deceiver man;
Heaven meant it as a blessing: she was plain.

Warrington, England
1816

●

ANONYMOUS

Beneath this silent stone is laid
A noisy antiquated maid
Who from her cradle talked to death,
And ne'er before was out of breath.

London, England
1750

ANNE HARRISON

Anne Harrison well known as NANNA
RAN DAN, who was chaste but no prude; & tho'
free yet no harlot. By Principle virtuous, by
Education a Protestant; her freedom made her
liable to censure, while her extensive charities made
her esteemed. Her tongue she was unable to
control, but the rest of her members she kept in
subjection.
After a life of 80 years thus spent, she died 1745.

Easingwald, England
1745

•

ANN MANN

Here lies Ann Mann;
She lived an old *Maid* and she died an old *Mann*.

Bath, England
c. 1750

DEBORAH KEENE

Here lieth interred
MRS. DEBORAH KEENE
late owner of the Manor of Braunton Arundell
in this parish
she was bapt'd Febr. the 24th 1627
Lived unmarried
and was bur'd Decem. the 31, 1694

Virginity was had in estimation,
And wont to be observed with veneration;
Above 'tis still so, single life is led:
In Heav'n none marry or are married,
But live Angelic lives, and virgins Crown'd
All with their coronets the Lamb surround.
This maiden landlady had one obtained
Wch. too much sought in marriage still retain'd
And now the inheritance undefiled obtain'd
Hoerdes posuere.

Braunton, England
1694

●

ARABELLA YOUNG

Here lies, returned to Clay
Miss Arabella Young,
Who on the first of May,
1771
Began to hold her tongue.

Pownal, Vermont
1771

LADY O'LOONEY

Here lies the body of
LADY · O'LOONEY
Great niece of *Burke*, commonly
Called the Sublime,
She was
Bland, passionate & deeply religious;
Also painted in watercolours,
And sent several pictures to the Exhibition.
She was the first cousin to Lady Jones.
And of such is the Kingdom of Heaven.

Pewsey, England
c. 1810

●

ANNIE SMITH

Here lyeth the body of Mrs. ANNIE Smith who departed
this Life octo the 28th in the yeare 1701
shee lived a maid and died aged 78.

Buckenhill, England
1701

●

DOROTHY CECIL

DOROTHY CECIL
Unmarried as yet

Wimbledon, England
c. 1900

MARGARET MOSELEY

MARGARET MOSELEY, ob. 1606 aet. 73

Under this stone a pearle is hid; what then
Search not; the pearle is Gods: and not for men.
A living pearle shee was whose lustre bright
Yielded all hers a long and sweet delight;
Noble by Birth by vertue more: in deed
More fruitfull then shee was in fruitfull Seed.
Much fuller then of yeares shee was of Grace
And now of Glory then of Grace shee was.

Wolverhampton, England
1606

●

ANNA LOVETT

Beneath this stone & not above it
Lie the remains of Anna Lovett;
Be pleased good reader not to shove it,
Least she should come again above it.
For 'twixt you & I, no one does covet
To see again this Anna Lovett.

[graveyard unknown] England
c. 1720

WILLISTON WINCHESTER

Williston Winchester
Son of Antipas & Lois Winchester
Born 1822 Died 1902
He never married
"Uncle Wid"
One of nature's noblemen, a quaint old
Fashioned, honest and reliable man.
An ideal companion for men and boys.
Delighted in hunting foxes and lining bees.

Marlboro, Vermont
1902

Sudden Death

•

The way someone died was always a favorite subject of epitaph writers, especially if the death was violent or unusual. Death by drowning was particularly commonplace, and worthy of remembrance. Those who were murdered often had the whole ordeal graphically retold on their tombstones, complete with warnings to the villains. A surprising number of the most creative epitaphs were written about death by lightning, always considered eminently suitable for posterity.

•

THOMAS HEMINGE

> The body that here buried lies
> By lightning's fell death's sacrifice
> To him Elijah's fate was given
> He rode on flames of fire to heaven.
> Then mourn no more Hees taken hence
> By the just hand of Providence.
> O God, the judgements of thy feat
> Are wondrous good & wondrous great
> Thy ways in all thy works appear
> As thunders loud, as lightnings clear.

Cornwall, England
1702

ALBERT FULLER

His death was occasioned by
an accidental blast of powder
on July 4th.

Putney, Vermont
1836

●

JOHN WRIGHT

Here I lie
No wonder I'm dead
For a broad wheeled Waggon
Went over my Head.
Grim Death took me
Without a Warning
I was Well at Night
And Dead in the Morning
15 March 1797

Sevenoaks, England
1797

●

ANN COLLINS

'Twas as she tript from Cask to Cask,
In a bung-hole quickly fell,
Suffocation was her task,
She had no time to say farewell.

King Stanley, England
1804

ROBERT BAXTER

All you that please these lines to read,
It will cause a tender heart to bleed.
I was murdered upon this fell,
And by a man I knew full well.
By bread and butter which he laid,
I, being harmless, was betrayed.
I hope he will rewarded be,
That laid the poison there for me.

Knaresdell, England
1796

•

JOHN PANNEL

Mr. John Pannel killed by a tree
In seventeen hundred & seventy three
When his father did come
He said Oh My Son
Your glass is run
Your work is done.

Halifax, Vermont
1773

73

RIC RICHARDS

To the Memory of
Ric Richards
Who by gangrene lost
a Toe afterwards a Leg
& lastly his Life
On the 7th day of April 1656

A Cruell Death to make 3
meales of one
To taste and taste till
all was gone
But know thou Tyrant
When the trumpe shall call
He'll find his feet
& stand when thou shalt call.

Banbury, England
1656

●

CAPTAIN THOMAS COFFIN

He's done a–catching cod
And gone to meet his God.

New Shoreham, Rhode Island
1842

NATHANIEL PARKE

In Memory of
Mr Nath. Parke
AEt 19, who on
21st March 1794
Being out a hunt-
ing and conceal'd
in a Ditch was
Casually shot by
Mr Luther
Frink.

Holyoke, Massachusetts
1794

●

DONALD ROBERTSON

Donald Robertson
Born 1st of January, 1765, died 4th of June, 1848
Aged 83 years
He was a peaceable quiet man, and to all appearance
a sincere Christian. His death was very much
regretted, which was caused by the stupidity of
Laurence Tulloch, of Clotherton, who sold him nitre
instead of Epsom salts, by which he was killed in the
space of 3 hours after taking a dose of it.

Shetland, Scotland
1848

In Memory of
Mary Maria
Wife of Wm. Dodd
who died Dec. 12th
AD 1847 aged 27
and
Of their children LOUISA
who died Dec. 12 1847
aged 9 months; & ALFRED
who died Jan. 3 AD 1848
aged 2 years & 9 months.

All victims to the neglect
of sanitary regulation
& specially referred to
in a recent lecture on
Health in this town.

Bilston, England
1847

ANONYMOUS

Here lies a Lewd Fellow
Who while he drew a Breath
In the midst of Life
Was in Quest of Death
Which he quickly obtained.

For it cost him his Life
For being in bed
With another man's wife.

[*Traditional, but undocumented*]

•

JOHN MARTIN

The Lord saw God, I was lopping off wood,
And down fell from the tree:
I met with a check, & I broke my neck,
And so Death lopped off me.

Ockham, England
1787

BENJAMIN ROWE

Serene and calm the mind in peace
His virtues shone with mild increase
In Memory of
Benjamin Rowe Esq
Who after a Life of great usefullness
& patiently enduring 4 years illness
with a dripsy underwent the Operation
of Tapping 67 times.
From his body was drawn 2385 pounds of water.
Quietly departed this Life the 28 day
of March Anno Domini 1790 in
the 71st year of his age.

Kensington, New Hampshire
1790

●

SARAH HALL

SARAH HALL
To the memory of a young maiden, who was
accidentally drowned December 24 1796
By her Lover
Nigh to the river Ouse, in York's fair city
Unto this pretty maid death shew'd no pity;
As soon as she'd her pail with water fill'd,
Came sudden death, and life like water spill'd.

York, England
1796

ELIZABETH WISE

Here lies
Elizabeth Wise
killed
by thunder
sent from heaven
in 16 hundred
and seventy seven

Edinburgh, Scotland
1677

●

JAMES BRUSH

To the memory of
MAJOR JAMES BRUSH
who was killed by the
accidental discharge of
a pistol by his orderly
14 APRIL 1831
Well done
good and faithul servant

Woolwich, England
1831

MERCY HALE

Here lies one wh
os life thrads
cut asunder she
was stroke dead
by a clap of thunder

Glastonbury, Connecticut
1719

●

SARAH LLOYD

SARAH LLOYD
On the 23rd of April 1800
In the 22nd year of her age
Suffered a just and ig-
nominious death
For admitting her
Abandoned seducer
In the dwelling-house of her
Mistress on the
3rd of October 1799
& becoming the instrument
In his hands of the crime of
Robbery & Housebreaking.

These were her last words:
MAY MY EXAMPLE BE A WARNING TO THOUSANDS.

Bury Saint Edmunds, England
1800

JOSEPH TALCOTT

> This monument is erected in
> Memory of Capt. Joseph Talcott
> Who was Casually Drowned in the
> Proud Waters of the Scungamug River
> On the 10th Day of June 1789
> In ye 62nd year of his age.

> *Coventry, Connecticut*
> *1789*

●

CALEB HOWE

> In Memory of Mr
> Caleb How a very
> Kind Companion who
> Was Killed by the Indea
> ns June the 27th
> 1755 in the 32nd year
> of his age his Wife Mrs
> Jemima How With 7
> Children taken Captive
> at the Same time

> Mr Caleb Howe Killed
> was by Indeans 1755

> *Hinsdale, New Hampshire*
> *1755*

MIRANDA BRIDGMAN

The rooms below flamed like a stove,
Anxious for those who slept above,
She ventured on ye trembling floor
She fell, she sunk, and rose no more.

Vernon, New Hampshire
1797

●

JOHN ADAM

Here lies John Adam, who received a thump
Right on the forehead from the Parish Pump,
Which gave him the quietus in the end
Though many doctors did his case attend.

Cheltenham, England
c. 1760

ABIAL LEDOYT PERKINS

Abial Ledoyt, son of
Jacob and Polly Perkins
who was drowned August 17, 1826
aged 13 years & 14 days

This blooming Youth in Health most fair
To his Uncle's Mill-pond did repaire,
Undressed himself and so plunged in
But never did come out again.

Plainfield, Vermont
1826

●

JOHN LAMB

On the 29th November,
A confounded piece of timber
Came down, bang slam,
And killed I, John Lamb.

Huntingdon, England
c. 1700

GILMAN SPAULDING

Mr Gilman Spaulding
Was kill'd with an axe
By an insane brother.

New Ipswich, New Hampshire
1842

●

MARY SINGLETON

Here lies interred the body of
MARY · SINGLETON
a young maiden of this parish
aged 9 years
Born of Roman Catholic parents
And virtuously brought up
Who being in the act of prayer
Repeating her Vespers
Was instantaneously kill'd by a flash of lightning
August 16th 1785

Bury Saint Edmunds, England
1785

JOSEPH GLEDOWING

Murdered near this town June 15, 1808
His murderers were never discovered

You villains! if this stone you see,
Remember that you murdered me!
You bruised my head and pierced my heart
Also my bowels did suffer part.

Workington, England
1808

●

JOHN FLYE

Here doth lye the bodie
of JOHN FLYE, who did die
By a stroke from a sky-rocket
Which hit him on the eye-socket.

Durness, Scotland
c. 1680

ELIZABETH HARRIS

Scared to the Memory of
Betsy Harris
Who died suddenly while contemplating
on the beauties of the moon
the 24th day of April 1831
in her 23rd Year

London, England
1831

●

MARY LOWDER

Here lies the body of Mary Ann Lowder
Who burst whilst drinking a seidlitz powder;
Called from this earth to her Heavenly rest
She should have waited till it effervesced.

Bruleigh, New Jersey
c. 1880

ROBERT C. WRIGHT

Robert C. Wright was born June 26, 1772. Died July 2nd 1815, by the bloodthursty hand of John Sweeny, Sr Who was massacre with the Nife, then a London Gun discharge a ball, penetrate the Heart, that give the mortal wound.

Appomattox, Virginia
1815

●

EDWARD PURDAY

Through a woman I received the wound
Which quickly brought my body to the ground.
Its sure in time that she will have her due,
The murdering hand God's vengeance will pursue.

One half Penny
The debt I owed that caused all the strife,
Was very small to cost me my sweet life.
She threatened to give me a mark,
Which made her cause look very dark.

Old Dalby, England
1733

RICHARD JARVIS

Here lies the body of Richard Jarvis
of Rickham, in this parish, who departed
this life the 25th day of May 1782. Aged 77.

Through poison strong he was cut off,
And brought to death at last.
It was by his apprentice girl
On whom there's a sentence past.
O may all people warning take,
For she was burned to a stake.

South Devon, England
1782

●

CHARLES RATHBONE

Here Charles Rathbone he doth lie
and by a misfortune he did die.
On the 17th of July.
1751

Shrewsbury, England
1751

JAMES HUNTER WRIGHT

James Hunter Wright was killed by falling from
the steeple of the Church.
At Jedburgh on 17th October, 1765

> Stop, traveller, as you go by,
>   I once had life and breath;
> But falling from a steeple high
> Swiftly passed through death.

Lilliesleaf, England
1765

●

REVEREND JOHN PINKERTON

After having spent a very Chearfull evening at
Balfour House with MR. BETHUNE and his
FAMILY he was found in the morning in his
bedroom sitting in a Chair by the Fireplace with
one stocking in his hand *Quite Dead.*

Markinch, Scotland
1784

ROGER MORTON

Here lies entombed one Roger Morton,
Whose sudden death was early brought on!
Trying one day his corns to mow off,
The razor slipped and cut his toe off!
The toe, or rather what it grew to;
An inflammation quickly flew to;
The parts then took to mortifying,
Which was the cause of Roger's dying.

Acton, England
c. 1770

●

FRANCES FLOOD

Stop Reader & wonder! see as strange as e'er was
known
My feet dript off from my body, in the midst of the
bone.
I had no surgeon for any help, but God Almighty's aid
On whom I always will rely & never be afraid;
Tho' here beneath intred they ly, corruption for to see:
Yet they shall rise & reunite to all Eternity.

Salford, England
1723

HENRY COOKE

In Memory of HENRY COOKE
7th Son of Thomas COOKE ESQ.
& Mrs. ABIGAIL his wife whose death
was caused by bathing, being taken
in a fit & immediately expired July
21st, 1789 Aged 15 years 3 Months &
11 Days

Martha's Vineyard, Massachusetts
1789

●

REUBEN ELDRIDGE

Stop! my friends as you pass by
And view the place in which I lie;
And learn how sudden life has fled
At night in health, next morning dead.

Harwich, Massachusetts
1824

●

ANNA HART

A person of little presumption
Died of a galloping consumption.

Greenwich, England
1815

HENRY BROWN

HENRY BROWN
Died 10 September 1794
aged 48 years.
It was an Imposthume
in my Breast,
That brought me to
eternal rest.

Hewelsfield, England
1794

●

SISTERS SAUNDERS

Rebecca Saunders, died Jan 6th 1837 aged 17 years
Barbara Saunders, died Jan 15th 1837 aged 15 years

With washing clothes from Sheffield bought,
Rebecca she the fever caught,
Which brought three more to this untimely end,
And no one could their assistance lend.

Ault Hucknall, England
1837

MARY SNELL

Poor MARY · SNELL, her's gone away
Her would if her could,
But her couldn't stay:
Her had sore legs and a baddish cough,
But her legs it were that carried her off.

Devonshire, England
c. 1800

●

ANONYMOUS

To all my friends I bid Adieu;
A more sudden death you never knew;
As I was leading the old mare to drink
She kicked and killed me quicker 'n a wink.

Oxford, New Hampshire
c. 1800

93

It's
Inevitable

•

Memento mori—remember you must die—is the most pervasive theme in epitaphs. It is the warning from beyond the grave, the reminder of mortality from those gone before to those reading the stones.

•

DR. ISAAC BARTHOLOMEW

He that was sweet to my Repose
Now is become a stink under my Nose.
This is said of me
So it will be said of thee.

Cheshire, Connecticut
1710

THOMAS WARNER

, Mr. Thomas Warner
who died
Sept. 4th 1787 aged 53

Our life hangs on a single thread
Which soon is cut & we are dead.
Then boast not reader of thy might
—Alive at noon & dead at night.

Essex, England
1787

●

LUCINA WILLCOX

In memory of miss
Lucina Willcox, who
Died May 7th 1800
aged 20 years.

Death is a debt
by nature due
I've paid my shot
And so must you.

Surrey, New Hampshire
1800

RICHARD SNELL

Stop, reader! and view this stone,
And ponder well where I have gone.
Then, pondering, take thou home this rhyme:
The grave next opened may be thine.

Cornwall, England
c. 1750

●

GEORGE SCOTT

In this vain world short was my stay,
And empty was my laughter;
I go before and lead the way
And thou comes jogging after.

Weatherall, England
1775

●

DANIEL EMERSON

The land I cleared is now my Grave.
Think well my Friends how you Behave.

Marlboro, New Hampshire
1829

97

ANONYMOUS

SHALL	WE	ALL	DIE?
WE	SHALL	DIE	ALL.
ALL	DIE	SHALL	WE?
DIE	WE	ALL	SHALL.

Cornwall, England
c. 1650

●

ELIZABETH THACHER

Naked as from the Earth we came,
and crept to life at first.
We to the Earth return again,
and mingle with our Dust.
The dear delights we here injoy,
and fondly call our own,
are but Short favours borrow'd now,
to be Repay'd anon.

Yarmouth, Massachusetts
1773

RICHARD WALTON

A shroude, a coffin, and a marble stone,
Are dead men's due; and may the living teach
That when to ripeness they are full growne,
Death will the best and fairest flowers reach.
For coulde a piouse life have stay'd death's force,
Hee yet hadd lived thatt's here a lifeless corse.

Blatonsbury, England
1609

●

WILLIAM DEERING

For me the world hath had its charms
And I've embraced them in my arms,
Courted its joys and sought its bliss
Although I knew the end was this.

Orient, Maine
1839

●

JOHN WARNER

I WARNER once was to myself
Now Warning am to thee
Both living, dying, dead I was,
See, then, thou warned be.

Ipswich, England
1641

JOHN ORGEN

As I was so be ye: as I am you shall be
What I gave, that I have
What I spent, that I had
Thus I count all my cost
That I left, that I lost.

London, England
1591

•

MARGARET TEASDALE

What I was once some may relate
What I am now is each one's fate;
What I shall be none can explain,
Till he that called, call again.

Upper Denton, England
1777

JOSEPH BAIN

Good peppell as you
pass by
I pray you on me cast
an I
For as you am so wounce
wous I
and as i am so must
you be
Therefor prepare to
follow me

Hastings, England
1751

●

DR. POLYCARPUS CUSHMAN

Vain censorius beings little know
What they must soon experience below.
Your lives are short, eternity is long;
O think of death, prepare & then begone.
Thus art & Nature's powers and charms
And drugs & receipts and forms
Yield all, at last, to greedy worms,
A despicable prey.

Bernardston, Massachusetts
1797

ROBERT GIPPES

ROBERT GIPPES, ob. 1624
Even dust as I am now
And thou in time shall be
Such one was I as thou:
Behold thyself by me.

Ipswich, England
1624

●

FRANCES A. LINNELL

There is no death.
What seems so is transition.
This is life of mortal breath
Is but a suburb of the life elysian,
Whose portal we call death.

Barnstable, Massachusetts
1881

●

RICHARD A. PRINE

Here lyeth Richard A. Prine
One thousand five hundred and eighty-nine.
Of March the 25th day,
And he that will die after him—may.

Derbyshire, England
1589

JOHN KERR

I dreamt that buried in my fellow clay
Close by a common beggar's side I lay;
Such a mean companion hurt my pride
And like a corpse of consequence I cried:
Scoundrel begone, and henceforth touch me not,
More manners learn, and at a distance rot.
Scoundrel, in still haughtier tones cried he,
Proud lump of earth, I scorn thy words and thee:
All here are equal, thy place now is mine;
This is my rotting place, and that is thine.

Providence, Rhode Island
1835

●

MRS. BEHN

Here lies a proof that wit can never be
Defence enough against mortality.

London, England
1689

●

JUDAH THACHER

Reader Stand stil & Speand a Tear
Think on the dust that Slumbers here
& When you think on ye State of me
Think on ye glass that runs for ye.

Yarmouth, Maine
1775

THOMAS HAWARD

Ashes of Ashes lie, on Ashes tread
Ashes engrav'd these words, which Ashes read,
Then what poor thing is Man, when every gust
Can blow his Ashes to their kindred dust?
More was intended, but a wind did rise,
And fill'd with Ashes both my mouth and eyes.

Kingston-upon-Thames, England
1655

●

JOHN LEWIS

Death is a debt to nature due
Which I have paid & so must you.
My friends tis is a waking call
For to be ready one & all,
As you are now so once was I
Now you may see what mortal worms we be.

Yarmouth, Maine
1756

LADY ELLEN TICHEBORNE

> Who lived (and now is dead)
> a life prepared for dying,
> Who died (and now she lyves)
> a death prepared for lyving
> So well she both profest
> That she in both is blest.

Aldershot, England
1606

•

JOHN DUNN

> This life's a stage where aged boys
> Cry once more for children's toys:
> The present is as was the past,
> Babes at first and babes at last.

Maddermarket, England
1813

Gluttons

●

"Eat, drink and be merry . . ." must have been the motto for many people, for most who follow were jolly souls who gave great glee to those who composed their epitaphs.

●

JOSEPH JONES

Here lies the bones
Of Joseph Jones
Who ate whilst he was able
But, once o'er fed
He dropt down dead
and fell beneath the table.
When from the tomb
To meet his doom,
He rises amidst sinners;
Since he must dwell
in Heav'n or Hell
Take him—which gives best dinners.

Wolverhampton, England
1690

JOHN RANDALL

Here old John Randall lies
Who counting from his tale
Lived three score years and ten
Such virtue was in Ale.
Ale was his meat,
Ale was his drink,
Ale did his heart revive:
And if he could have drunk his Ale
He still have been alive:
But he died Januar five
1699.

Great Wallford, England
1699

●

DONALD JONES

Here lies the bones
o' *Donald Jones*
The wale o' men
for eating scones,
Eating scones
and drinking yill,
Till his last moans
He took his fill.

Isle of Skye, Scotland
c. 1775

REV. JOHN TYRWITT

Here lays
John Tyrwitt
A learned Divine
He died in a fit
Through drinking Port Wine
Died 3rd, April 1828, Aged 59

Malta
1828

●

GEORGE MUTTON

Sacred to the memory of GEORGE MUTTON
Who surfeited himself with eating bacon;
It's a very surprising thing to me,
That mutton and bacon can't agree.

North Buckland, England
c. 1750

●

MRS. SHUTE

Here lies, cut down like unripe fruit,
The wife of *Deacon* AMOS SHUTE.
She died of drinking too much coffee,
Anny dominy eighteen forty.

Windsor, Connecticut
1840

SIDNEY SNYDER

The wedding day,
decided was,
The wedding wine
provided;
But ere the day did
come along
He drunk it up and
died, did.
Ah Sidney! Ah Sidney!

Providence, Rhode Island
1823

●

THOMAS DAVIES

In memory of THOMAS DAVIES, late of
Langley, Gent. who departed this Life
April 14, 1760 aged 31
Good natur'd, generous, bold & free,
He always was in Company.
He lived his Bottle & his friend
Which brought upon soon his latter end.

Stanton Lacy, England
1760

DANIEL LAMBERT

In remembrance of that prodigy of nature, DANIEL
LAMBERT, a native of Leicester, who was possessed of
an excellent & convivial mind, & in personal greatness
he
had no competitor. He measured three feet one inch
round
the leg; nine feet four inches round the body,
and weighed
52 st. 11 lbs. [739 lbs.]. He departed this life 21st of
June 1809 aged 39 years.

As a testimony of respect, this Stone is erected by his
friends
in Leicester.

Stamford, England
1809

●

REBECCA FREELAND

She drank good ale, good punch and wine
And lived to the age of 99.

Edwalton, England
1741

WILLIAM SYMONS

Here lies my corpse, who was the man
That loved a sop in the dripping pan;
But now believe me I am dead
See her the pan stands at my head.
Still for sops till the last I cried
But could not eat, & so I died.
My neighbours, they perhaps will laugh,
When they do read my epitaph.
                    1753 William Symons

Newmarket, England
1753

●

CLAPPER WATTS

Who lies here?—who do'e think?
Why old Clapper Watts, if you' give him some drink.
Give a dead man drink, for why?
Why, when he was alive, he was always adry.

Leigh Delamere, England
c. 1670

●

HENRY HARPER

Drink's the curse of the land, say I
Through drink it was that I did die.
Against all spirits take a solemn vow:
Had I done so, I'd been living now.

Beccles, England
1801

JOHNNY COLE

Here lies Johnny Cole
Who died, on my soul,
After eating a plentiful dinner.
While chewing his Crust,
He was turned to Dust,
With crimes undigested—poor sinner.

[graveyard unknown] England
c. 1720

●

PATRICK WARD

Beneath this stone here lieth one
That still his friends did please,
To Heaven I hope is surely gone
To enjoy eternal ease.
He drank, he sang, whilst here on Earth
Lived happy as a lord,
And now he hath resigned his breath—
God rest him, Paddy Ward!

Mayne, Ireland
1785

Soldiers And Sailors

•

Service to one's country was a lifetime occupation, and certainly worth commemorating. While the noblest way to die was in battle, any death of a soldier or sailor was memorialized—often recounting stories lost to history, sometimes with humorous results.

•

JOHN MACPHERSON

Here Lies
John Macpherson
Who was a
very peculiar
person
He stood
six foot two
without his shoe
And was slew
at Waterloo.

Dumfries, Scotland
1814

CAPTAIN JOHN DYER

Whom neither Sword nor Gunn in War
Could slay, in Peace a cough did marr.
'Gainst Rebels He and Lust and Sin
Fought the good Fight, died Life to win.

Glastonbury, England
1670

●

WILLIAM RICHARD PHELPS

William Richard Phelps
(Late Boatswain of H.M.S. Invinsible)
He accompanied Lord Anson in his
cruise round the world
and died April 21st 1789 AD

When I was like you
For years not a few,
On the ocean I toil'd
On the line I boil'd
In Greenland I've shiver'd
Now from hardships deliver'd
Capsized by old Death
I surrender my breath
And now I lie snug
As a bug in a rug.

Liverpool, England
1789

CAPTAIN WILLIAM H. BURGESS

Capt. Wm. H. Burgess
Master of Ship Challenger
died at Sea Dec 1856
aged 27 Y'rs. 9 mo's.
& 16 days
Temporarily buried
at Valparaiso
S.A. Dec. 14

Bourne, Massachusetts
1856

●

JOHN COLLINS

Here rest the remains
of
JOHN COLLINS
A Serjeant of the
ROYAL MARINES
He was one of England's
Gallant Sons
Before Sebastopol was
blown to smithereens
By a charge from the
Russian guns.
October 17, 1854

Therpia, Turkey
1854

HARRY ROCKWELL

Landsmen or sailors,
For a moment avast,
Poor Jack's topsail
is laid to the mast.
The worms gnaw his timbers
His vessel's a wreck,
When the last whistle sounds
He'll be up on deck.

East Hampton, Connecticut
1883

●

CHARLES CARR

I've mock'd the storm
Outrid the wave
And found harbour in the grave;
With joy forsook this earthly clod,
And flew into the arms of God.

Westham, England
1782

JOSEPH P. BRAINERD

Joseph P. Brainerd
  A Brave Soldier
Joseph Partridge
Brainerd, Son of
Joseph H. Brainerd
and his wife Fanny Part
ridge, a conscientious,
faithful, brave Union
Soldier, was born on the
27th day of June 1840,
graduated from the
University of Vermont
in August 1862, enlisted
into Co. L. of the Vermont
Calvery, was wounded
and taken prisoner by the
Rebels in the Wilderness,
May 5, 1864, was sent to
Andersonville Prison
Pen in Georgia where he died
on the 11th day of Sept. 1864
entirely and wholly neglected by
President Lincoln and murdered
with impunity by the Rebels,
with thousands of our loyal
Soldiers by Starvation, Privation,
Exposure and Abuse.

St. Albans, Vermont
1864

THOMAS CORBISHLEY

Reader take notice
That on ye 12 Feby 1760
Tho. Corbishley
A brave veteran Dragoon
Here went to his quarters
But remember that when
The trumpet calls
He'll out and march again.

Gawsworth, England
1760

●

JAMES GREEN

To the memory of
JAMES · GREEN
Able Seaman
Aged 25
A block fell on his head
From aloft & killed him dead
Erected by his messmates, as a
Silent tribute to his memory.

Thespia, Turkey
1855

JOHN REDDISH

JOHN REDDISH Esq.
Lieut. Colonel in the army
died 17th May 1717
aged 69
When he sought death
with sword & shield

Death was afraid
to meet him in the field
But when his weapons he had
laid aside
Death, like a coward, stoke him
& he died.

Isle of Man, England
1717

●

THOMAS TAYLOR

Repent! Repent! while you have time,
Here I lie cut off in my prime,
Tom Taylor,
A Sailor,
Aged 79.

Cork, Ireland
c. 1720

THOMAS THETCHER

To the memory of Thomas Thetcher
Grenadier in the Hants. Militia,
who died of a violent fever contracted
by drinking small beer when hot,
on the 12th May, 1764

Here sleeps in peace a Hampshire grenadier,
Who caught his death by drinking cold small beer,
Soldiers be wise from his untimely fall,
And when you're hot drink strong or not at all.

An honest soldier never is forgot.
Whether he die by musket or by pot.

Winchester, England
1764

●

JOHN DUNCH

JOHN DUNCH
CAPTAIN MARINER
Though boreas' blasts and Neptune's waves
Have toss'd me to & fro:
In spite of both by Heaven's decree,
Harbour I here below
Where I do now at anchor ride
With many of our fleet:
Yet once again I must set saile,
Our ADMIRAL CHRIST to meet.

London, England
c. 1780

ANNE SPRAGGE

Sacred to posterity.
In a vault, near this place, lies the body of
ANNE, the only daughter of
EDWARD CHAMBERLAYNE, LL.D.
Born in London, January 20, 1667,
Who,
For a considerable time, declined the matrimonial
state,
And scheming many things
Superior to her sex and age,
On the 30th of June, 1690,
And under the command of her brother,
With arms and in the dress of a man,
She approv'd herself a true *Virago*,
By fighting undaunted in a fire ship against the
French,
Upwards of six hours,
She might have given us a race of heroes,
Had not premature fate interposed.
She returned safe from the naval engagement,
And was married, in some months after, to
JOHN SPRAGGE, Esq.
With whom she lived half a year extremely happy,
But being delivered of a daughter, she died
A few days after,
October 30, 1692.

This monument, to his most dear and affectionate
wife, was erected by her most disconsolate
husband.

London, England
1692

WILLIAM FRENCH

WILLIAM FRENCH

The First American Killed in the Revolution
                    March 13, 1775
Here William French his body lies.
For murder His blood for vengeance cries.
King George the Third his Tory crew,
That with a ball his head shot threw.
For Liberty and his Country's good
He lost his life His dearest blood.

Westminster, Vermont
1775

•

CHIEF ORONO OF THE PENOBSCOT INDIANS

Safe lodged within his blanket here below
Lies the last relics of Old Orono.
Wore down with care, he in a trice
Exchanged his Wigwam for a Paradise.

Old Town, Maine
1801

Good
Riddance

•

Here is a case of those who lived getting final revenge on the dead. There is no question that someone was glad to see each of the following people go. So glad, in fact, that they paid for the stone to say so.

•

WILLIAM WISEMAN

> Here lies the body of W. W.
> He comes no more to trouble U, trouble U.
> Where he's gone or how he fares,
> Nobody knows & nobody cares.

Walcot, England
1847

PATRICK STEEL

Here lies Pat Steel,
That's very true!
Who was he! What was he!
What's that to you?
He lies here, because he
Is dead—nothing new.

Cork, Ireland
c. 1750

●

FRANCES CHERRY

HIC · JACET · PECCATORUM · MAXIMUS ·
[Here lies the greatest of sinners.]

Shottesbrook, England
1773

MARY S. HOYT

> She lived—what more can be said:
> She died—and we all know she's dead.

Bradford, Vermont
1836

●

BOB BARRES

> Hurrah! Me boys at the Parson's fall,
> For if he'd lived he'd 'a buried us All.

Taibach, South Wales
c. 1790

●

NICHOLAS SANFORD

NICHOLAS SANFORD.
He was
A patterne for townesmen, whom we may enrole,
For at his own charge this towne hee freed of tole.

Wisbech, England
1638

JONATHAN TILTON

Here lies the body of Jonathan Tilton
whose friends reduced him to a skeleton.
They robbed him out of all he had
and now rejoice that he is dead.

Chilmark, Massachusetts
1837

●

WILLIAM WRAY

Here lyeth wrapt in Clay
the Body of William Wray
I have no more to say.

London, England
c. 1700

●

ANONYMOUS

Those who care for him while living
will know whose body is buried here.
To others it does not matter.

Hartford, Connecticut
1882

JOHN SHORE

> Here lies JOHN SHORE
> I say no more;
> Who was alive
> In sixty-five.

Wrexham, England
1765

●

JOHN RACKET

> Here lies *John Racket*
> In his wooden jacket,
> He kept neither horses nor mules;
> He lived like a hog,
> He died like a dog,
> And left his money to fools.

Woodton, England
c. 1780

●

ROBERT BURROWS

> Poems and epitaphs are but stuff
> Here lies ROBERT BURROWS, that's enough.

Bedlington, England
c. 1830

? COLEMAN

If *Heaven* be pleas'd, when Sinners cease to sin,
If *Hell* be pleas'd, when Souls are damn'd therein;
If *Earth* be pleas'd, when its rid of a Knave;
Then *all* are pleas'd, for *Coleman's* in his grave.

London, England
c. 1670

●

THOMAS CLAY

What though no mournful kindred stand
Around the solemn bier,
No parents wring the trembling hand,
Or drop the silent tear.

To costly oak adorned with art
My weary limbs enclose,
No friends impart a winding sheet
To deck my last repose.

North Wingfield, England
1794

●

RICHARD HIND

Here lies the Body of RICHARD HIND,
Who was neither ingenious, sober, or kind.

Cheshunt, England
c. 1800

SARAH THOMAS

SARAH THOMAS
is dead
And that's enough.
The candle is out
Also the snuff.
Her soul is in Heaven
You need not fear;
And all that's left
Is interred here.

Keysville, New York
c. 1850

●

JOHN YOUNG

JOHN YOUNG
Those who knew him best deplored him most.

[unverified]

REVEREND JOHN MAWER

This monument rescues from oblivion the remains of the Rev. John Mawer, D.D., late vicar of this parish, who died Nov. 18, 1763, aged sixty; as also of Hannah Mawer, his wife, who died Dec. 22, 1766, aged seventy-two; buried in the Chancel. They were persons of eminent worth. The Doctor was descended from the Royal family of Mawer, and was inferior to none of his illustrious ancestors in personal merit, being the greatest linguist this country ever produced. He was able to speak and write 22 languages, and particularly excelled in the Eastern tongues in which he proposed to His Royal Highness Frederick, Prince of Wales, to whom he was firmly attached, to propagate the Christian religion in the Abyssinian Empire; a great and noble design, which was frustrated by the death of this excellent prince, to the great mortification of this excellent person, whose merit, meeting with no reward in this world, will, it is to be hoped, receive it in the next, from that Being which justice only can influence.

Middleton, England
1766

? BALL

Here I lie, My name is BALL—
I lived—I died, despised by all.
And now I cannot chew my crust,
I'm gone back to ancient dust.

Wiltshire, England
c. 1620

●

ABRAHAM NEWLAND

Beneath this stone old Abr'am lies:
Nobody laughs and nobody cries:
Where he's gone or how he fares,
Nobody knows and nobody cares.

London, England
1807

●

EDWARD HIDE

Here lies the body of Edward Hide
We laid him here because he died.
We had rather
It had been his father;
If it had been his sister
We should no have missed her.
But since 'tis honest Ned
No more shall be said.

Storrington, England
1750

Nipped In The Bud

•

Perhaps the saddest of all epitaphs are those written for children. Infant mortality was extremely high, and even though almost every family lost at least one child early, they still seemed to be the most painful of losses. It is interesting that some families employed a touch of humor—albeit bittersweet—to help them ease their grief.

•

EMMA AND MARIA LITTLEBOY

Emma & Maria
Littleboy
the twin children
of George & Emma
Littleboy of Hornsey
who died
July 16th 1837

Two littleboys lie here
yet strange to say
these *little boys* are girls

London, England
1837

EZRA THAYER JACKSON

What did the Little hasty sojourner
find so forbidding & disgustful in
our upper world to occasion its
precipitant exit.

Plymouth, Massachusetts
1783

●

JOHN MAGHI

to the memory of
JOHN MAGHI
An incomparable boy,
Who, thro' the unskilfulness of the midwife,
On the 21st day of December, 1532
Was translated from the womb to the tomb.

[graveyard unknown] England
1532

ELIZABETH STREVEN

In memory of
Elizabeth Streven
Who resign'd her soul to Heav'n
Her years were exactly seven
Died 9th May 17 hunder'd & 11.

Shrewsbury, England
1711

●

? LEISTON

In a small grave here little LEISTON lies
Who bore a great resemblance with the Skies
For as the Sun in twelve month race doth gett
To the end of's course, twice six this saw & sett.

Mereworth, England
1641

ELIZABETH EMMA THOMAS

She had no fault save what travellers give the moon:
Her light was lovely, but she died too soon.

Islington, England
1808

●

PALMER QUADRUPLETS

In Memory of four infants
of Jacamiah & Mercy Palmer
was born alive at one birth
& died Nov. 25, 1795

Four twen infants they are dead
And laid in one silent grave
Christ took small infants in his arms
Such infants he will save.

Danby Four Corners, Vermont
1795

●

WIFE AND DAUGHTER OF DR. H. WILKENSON

Here lies mother & babe, both without sins,
Next birth will make her and her infant twins.

Great Milton, England
1654

F. W. JACKSON

Heav'n knows What man
He might have made But we;
He died a most rare boy

Plymouth, Massachusetts
1799

●

FRANCES AND PETER WISELY

In *one* house they were nursed & fed
Beneath one mother's eye;
One fever laid them on *one* bed
On *one* bed both their spirits fled
and in *one* grave they lie.

Insch, New Brunswick, Canada
1843

●

HENRY G. BROWN

How soon I was cut down,
when innocent at play,
The wind it blew a ladder down,
and took my life away.

Baldock, England
1861

ELIZABETH SKOTTOWE

ELIZABETH SKOTTOWE aet. 3
Stay: shee'll awake 'ere long, then cease to weepe,
The Damosell is not dead, but shee's asleepe,
  she (like her Sister) did but take a Taste
Of Mortal Life, then breathed it out in haste;
  In expectation of the ONE in *Three*.

Little Melton, England
1656

●

SON OF TIMOTHY HOSKINS, JR.

This rose was sweet awile
Now it is odour vile.

Westmoreland, New Hampshire
1813

●

A. S. B.

The cup of life just to her lips she prest;
Found its taste bitter & denied the rest,
Averse, then turning from the light of day
She softly sighed her little life away.

Beckington, England
1845

JOHN WEBSTER

Ye little children that survey,
The emblemed wheel that crush'd me down,
Be cautious, as you careless play,
For shafts of death fly thick around.
Still rapid drives the car of time,
Whose wheels one day shall crush you all;
The cold low bed that now is mine,
Will soon be that of great and small.

Islington, England
1809

●

GEORGE GELSTON

George, Son of
Doctr. Roland Gelston
and Love his wife
Who died of the putrid
Sour throat Jan. 20, 1795

Nantucket, Massachusetts
1795

GILBERT CAMFIELD

In this dust lyeth the body of Gilbert ye elder
twin of Benjamin & Martha Camfield

Eager to live he grow did first,
Into this world by sin accurs'd
But being born he live
Not ful 3 months he tryd
Lik'd not the place & dyd.

Whitwell, England
1669

●

WILLIAM HASELWOOD

The Hasel nut oft children crops
good HASELWOOD in childhood lopps
Then, Parent, yield, God says, hee's mine,
And took him hence say not hee's thine.

Ipswich, England
1643

JOHN BOYSE

Blest was the Prophet in his Heavenly Shade
But oh! how soon did his umbrella fade.

Like our frail Bodies which being born of Clay
Spring in a Night and wither in a Day.

Devon, England
1684

●

CAROLINE NEWCOMB

She tasted of life's bitter Cup
Refus'd to drink the Portion up
But turned her little head aside
Disgusted with the taste and died.

Martha's Vineyard, Massachusetts
1812

●

GEORGE HILL

Against his will
Here lies GEORGE HILL,
Who from a cliff
Fell down quite stiff.
When it happened is not known,
Therefore not mentioned on this stone.

Thanet, England
c. 1775

ANONYMOUS

Mammy and I together lived
Just two years and a half
She went first—I followed next
The cow before the calf.

Worcester, England
c. 1750

●

PRISCILLA PARKER

Sweet Babe
She glanced into our world to see
A sample of our misery.
Then turned away her languid eye
To drip a tear or two and die.

Groveland, Massachusetts
1817

●

ANONYMOUS

The Little Hero that lies here
Was conquered by the Diarreah.

Portland, Maine
c. 1800

MILLA GAYLORD

Soon ripe
Soon rotten
Soon dead
But not forgotten

*Hamden, Connecticut
1806*

●

WILLIAM BARY

Opened my eyes, took a peep,
Didn't like it, went to sleep

*Petersborough, New Hampshire
1823*

●

SARAH BLOOMFIELD

Here lyeth ye body of
SARAH BLOOMFIELD
aged 74
Cut off in blooming youthe; we can but pity.

*Yarmouth, England
c. 1675*

Come Again?

•

Sometimes attributable to mistakes by the stonecutter, sometimes to a misuse or misunderstanding of the language, these startling epitaphs all invite repeated readings. But many times the lines meant exactly what they said—which is the most surprising of all.

•

JAMES VERNON, ESQ.

Here lies the body of James Vernon, Esq., only
surviving son of Admiral Vernon.
Died 23rd July 1723.

*Plymouth, England
1723*

THOMAS NICOLS

Here lie the remains of Thomas Nicols who died in
Philadelphia, March, 1753. Had he lived he would
have been buried here.

Kir-Keel, Scotland
1753

●

JOHN ELDRED

Here lies the body of John Eldred
At least he will be here when he is dead;
But now at this time he is alive,
The 14th of August, sixty five.

Oxfordshire, England
1765

JOHN HIGLEY

Here lies JOHN HIGLEY, whose father and mother were
drowned on their passage from America. Had both
lived
they would have been buried here.

Belturbet, Ireland
c. 1750

●

JAMES BAKER

O cruel Death, how could you be so unkind,
To take him before & leave me behind?
You should have taken both of us if either,
Which wou'd have been more pleasing to the survivor.

Birmingham, England
1781

●

GEORGE AND ISABEL GUTHRIE

Here lyes the Bodeys of
GEORGE YOUNG & ISABEL GUTHRIE
And all of their posterity for more than fifty years
backward.

Montrose, New Brunswick, Canada
1757

NICHOLAS ROUND

Here lies the body of Nicholas Round
Who was lost at sea & never found.

Great Yarmouth, England
c. 1790

•

JOHN AND EDWARD TOPHAM

Reader from this monument may gather
JOHN TOPHAM was one EDWARD TOPHAM's father.
And what's more strange, we find, upon this stone,
That EDWARD TOPHAM was JOHN TOPHAM's Son.

New Windsor, England
1692

•

JOHN THOMAS

Here lies John Thomas
And his three children dear
Two buried at Oswestry,
And one here.

Llanmynech, Wales
c. 1720

ANDREW ROBERTSON

Here lies the corpse of Andrew Robertson
Present Deacon-Convener of Weavers in this Burgh.
Who died 13th July 1745.

Dumfermline, New Brunswick, Canada
1745

●

JOHN MacFARLANE

Erected to the memory of
John MacFarlane
Drowned in the Water of Leith
By a few affectionate friends.

Edinburgh, Scotland
c. 1800

●

WALTER DAVIS

WALTER DAVIS
DIED
FEB. 7th BERRIED
FEB th9
1930

New Orleans, Louisiana
1930

JOHN PARKER, JAMES HAMILTON, & CHRISTOPHER STRANG

Stay passenger, take notice
What thou reads
At Edinboro be our bodies
Here our heads.

Our right hands stood at Lanark
These we want
Because with them we sware
The Covenant.

Hamilton, New Brunswick, Canada
1666

Died With
Their Boots On

•

There is something nearing affection for those who died in the act of committing, or because they committed, a crime. Occasionally there is a warning to others who might be tempted to try the same thing; but usually the facts are stated and all appears to be forgiven, once the epitaph has set the record straight.

•

LESTER MOORE

HERE LIES
Lester Moore
four slugs
from a 44
no less
no more

Tombstone, Arizona
c. 1880

UNKNOWN MAN

unknown man shot in
the Jennison & Gallup Co.'s store
while in the act of burglarizing
the safe Oct. 13, 1905.
(Stone bought with money
found on his person.)

Sheldon, Vermont
1905

●

PARKER HALL

Here lies Parker Hall & what is rarish,
He was born, bred & hanged in St. Thomas's Parish.

Oxford, England
c. 1700

JOHN SMITH

In memory ov
John Smith, who met
wierlent death near this spot,
18 hundred and 40 too. He was shot
by his own pistill
It was not one of the new kind
but a old-fashioned
brass barrel, and of such is the
Kingdom of Heaven.

Sparta, California
1842

●

ANONYMOUS

HE CALLED
BILL SMITH
A LIAR.

Cripple Creek, Colorado
c. 1875

155

A. J. ALLEN, LOUIS CURRY, JAMES HALL

A. J. ALLEN   LOUIS CURRY   JAS. HALL
age 35   age 29   age 19

Here lies the bodies of Allen, Curry, and Hall.
Like other thieves they have their rise, decline and fall.
On yon pine tree they hung till dead,
And here they found a lonely bed.
Then be a little cautious how you gobble horses up,
For every horse you pick up here, adds sorrow to your cup.
We're bound to stop this business, or hang you to a man,
For we've hemp and hand enough in town to hang the whole
DAMN CLAN

Rapid City, South Dakota
1877

●

DAN DOUD, REX SAMPLE, TEX HOWARD, BILL DELANEY, DAN KELLEY

DAN DOUD

REX SAMPLE

TEX HOWARD

BILL DELANEY

DAN KELLEY

LEGALLY
HANGED
MAR. 8, 1884

Tombstone, Arizona
1884

156

GEORGE JOHNSON

GEORGE JOHNSON
HANGED BY MISTAKE!

Tombstone, Arizona
c. 1880

●

J. B. HICKOK

Wild Bill
J. B. Hickok
Killed by the assassin
Jack M'Call
In Deadwood, Black Hills
Aug. 2d 1876

Pard, we wil meet
again in the Happy
Hunting Ground
To part no more,
Goodbye
Colorado
Charlie
C. H. Utter

Deadwood, Colorado
1876

THOMAS KEMP

Here lies the body of *Thomas Kemp*
Who lived by the wool and died by the hemp
There was nothing would suffice the glutton
But with the fleece to steal the mutton
Had he but worked and lived uprighter
He'd ne'er been hung for a sheep-biter.

[graveyard unknown] England
c. 1700

Glad
To Go

•

Occasionally life was so depressing or painful that the afterlife looked pretty good. These poor people welcomed whatever came after.

•

LYDIA SNOW

> Gladly I quit this vile, decrepit clay,
> To rise in endless youth, in endless day.

Wellfleet, Massachusetts
1816

REVEREND WILLIAM GOODWIN

Here lies
the learned and facetious
Reverend WILLIAM GOODWIN
Fellow of Eaton College and
Vicar of St. Nicholas, who died
in June 1747. These written for
himself.

Here lies a head that often ach'd;
Here lie two hands that always shak'd
Here lies a brain of odd conceit;
Here lies a heart that often beat;
Here lie two eyes that daily wept,
And in the night but seldom slept;
Here lies a tongue that whining talk'd;
Here lie two feet that feebly walk'd;
Here lie the midriff, and the breast,
With loads of indigestion prest;

Here lies the liver full of bile,
That ne'er secreted proper chyle;
Here lie the bowels, human tripes,
Tortur'd with wind, and twisting gripes;
Here lies that livid dab, the spleen,
The source of life's sad tragic scene;
That left side weight that clogs the blood,
And stagnates nature's circling flood;
Here lie the nerves, so often twich'd,
With painful cramps, and poignant stitch;
Here lies the back, oft rack'd with pains,
Corroding kidnies, loins and reins;

Here lies the skin *per* scurvy fed,
With pimples, and eruptions red;
Here lies the man, from top to toe,
That fabric fam'd for pain and woe;
He caught a cold, but colder death,
Compress'd his lungs and top't his breath;
The organs could no longer go,
Because the bellows ceas'd to blow.

Thus I dissect this honest friend,
Who ne'er till death was at wit's end;
For want of spirits here he fell;
With higher spirits let him dwell,
In future state of peace and love,
Where just men's perfect spirits move.

Bristol, England
1747

●

HENRY CLAY BARNEY

My life's been hard
And all things show it,
I always thought so,
And now I know it.

Guilford, Vermont
1915

RUSSELL STOWELL

Let no one stand behind my grave,
Now that I am called to rest,
Nor shed a tear that I am gone,
For what I need is rest.

Rest from the weary load of care,
Rest for the wearing pain:
For Death shall ever be to me
An everlasting gain.

I know the road was bright and fair
Or once it seemed to be.
But it has changed so much of late,
It has few charms for me.

Chesterfield, New Hampshire
1875

ELIJAH OLDFIELD

Here is the wardrobe of my dusty clothes
Which hands divine shall brush & make so gay
That my immortal soule shall put them on
And wear the same upon my Wedding Daye;
In which attire my Lord shall me convoy,
Then to the lodginge of Eternal joy.

Chipping Sodbury, England
1642

●

JANE KITCHEN

Here lies JANE KITCHEN
Who when her glass was spent,
She kickt up her heels
And away she went.

Bury Saint Edmunds
c. 1750

●

CATHERINE WATTS

Who hopes to sing without a sob
The Anthem ever new
And gladly bids the dusty globe
And vain delights adieu.

Edmonton, England
1796

JOHN H. COOPER

In Memory of
John Heath Cooper of this
town Never know to be parilised
by any Man in his profession

he had a Natural Genius in many
other things but Leaving this sinful world in
hopes of a better

He died Octbr ye 21st 1772 Aged 54
When young he was beloved
By all that knew him
But growing old & poor
They all forsook him
But God his Father & his Friend
Did still regard him to the end.

Ledbury, England
1772

●

MRS. SARAH NEWMAN

Pain was my portion,
Physic was my food
Groans my devotion,
Drugs did me no good.
Christ was my physician
Knew what way was best,
To ease me of my pain,
He took my soul to rest.

Clerkenwell, England
c. 1700

164

TEAGUE O'BRIEN

Here at length I repose
And my spirit at aise is,
With the tips of my toes & the point of my nose
Turned up to the roots of the daisies.

Tipperary, Ireland
c. 1750

●

REBECCA ROGERS

An house he hath, 'tis made of such good fashion,
The tenant ne'er shall pay for reparation;
Nor will his landlord ever raise the rent,
Nor turn him out of doors for non-payment;
From chimney-money too, this house is free,
To such a house who would not tenant be?
Erected 1688.

Folkestone, England
1688

●

ANONYMOUS

Cold is my bed, but ah I love it,
For colder are my friends above it.

Chicago, Illinois
1859

John L. Jones
1811–1875

I came without my own consent,
Lived a few years much discontent,
At human errors grieving.
I ruled myself by reason's laws,
But got contempt and not applause
Because of disbelieving.

For nothing me could e'er convert
To faith some people did assert,
Alone could gain salvation.
But now the grass does me enclose
The superstitious will suppose
I'm doomed to Hell's damnation.

But as to that they do not know;
Opinions oft from ignorance flow,
Devoid of some foundation.
Tis easy men should be deceived
When anything by them's believed,
Without a demonstration.

West Ripley, Massachusetts
1875

Better Late Than Never

•

Longevity has always been admired, especially during times when life expectancy wasn't very long. While some of these people actually lived as long as their epitaphs claim, it seems clear that occasionally the stonecutter may have embellished a little.

•

STEPHEN RUMBOLD

Here lyes *Stephen Rumbold*
He lived to the age of an hundred and one
Sanguine and Strong
An hundred to one you don't live so long.

Brightwell-Baldwin, England
1687

MARY BUEL

Here lies the body of Mrs. Mary wife
of Dea. John Buel Esq. She died
Nov. 4 1768 AEat. 90
Having had 13 children
101 grand-children
274 great-grand-children
49 great-great-grand-children
410 Total. 336 survived her.

Litchfield, Connecticut
1768

●

JOHN REES

Here lieth the body of
JOHN REES
Who departed this Life
Octr. the 17th 1824
Aged
249 Years
Reader,
Prepare to meet thy God

Amroth, England
1824

JOSEPH LEE

Aged 103 years
Joseph Lee is dead & gone
We ne'er shall see him more
He used to wear an old drab coat
All buttoned down before.

Chepstow, England
1825

●

ELIZABETH FARREN

Elizabeth Farren, Aged 102 Years
She was a woman of very shrewd understanding
& a remarkable instance of healthy longevity,
In her hundred & first year she threaded her needle
without spectacles
and regularly walked a mile & a half to church
until a very short time before her death
on 29th February 1832

Hendon, England
1832

August 7th 1714
MARY
The wife of JOSEPH YATES
of Lizard Common within
this parish,
was buried
Aged 127 Years.

She walked to LONDON
just after the Fire in 1666
was hearty & strong at
120 years
and married a 3rd husband
at 92

Shifnal, England
1714

ELIZA SHAW

This stone is sacred
To the Memory of
ELIZA · SHAW
Who died Nov. 10th 1820
Aged 118 years
She lived six reigns, & enjoyed excellent
Health until a few hours previous to her death.

Tickhill, England
1820

●

EBENEZER SCOTT

Grandfather
the first white male born in Bernardston,
Mass. Was taken with his mother and two brothers
by the Indians, carried to Quebec, sold to the
French when he was 8 years old. Returned to his
father. Served in the Revolution—drew a pension.

Vernon, Vermont
1826

MARY ELLIS

Here lies the body of Mary Ellis & Lydia, his wife, of this
parish. She was a virgin of virtuous character & most
promising homes. She died on the 3rd of June 1609.
Aged one hundred & nineteen

Leigh, England
1609

●

JOHN BAILES

Here under lyeth
JOHN · BAILES Born in this
Town he was above 126
years old & had his hearing
Sight & Memory to ye last
He lived 3 Centurys,
& was buried ye 14th of Apr
1706.

Northampton, England
1706

Slaves

●

It is unfortunate that more epitaphs of slaves have not been preserved, but it is not surprising, considering that even a simple burial has always been expensive, and stone markers out of the reach of many. But the few remaining present unique views of a personal history, and are well worth reading.

●

CAESAR

Here lies the best of slaves
Now turning into Dust
Caesar, the Ethiopian craves
A place amoung the Just.
His faithful soul is fled
To realms of heavenly light,
And by the blood that Jesus shed
Is changed from Black to White.

Jany 15 he quitted this stage
In the 77th year of his age.
1780

North Attleboro, Massachusetts
1780

NANCY WILLIAMS

In memory of Nancy Williams
A faithful (African) servant in the
family of Rev. F. Freeman, died
Nov. 30, 1831, aged 25 years.

Honor and shame from no conditions rise:
Act well your part—there all honour lies.

Plymouth, Massachusetts
1831

●

AMOS AND VIOLATE FORTUNE

Sacred to the Memory of Amos Fortune
who was born free in Africa
a slave in America, he purchased
liberty, professed Christianity,
lived reputably, died hopefully,
Nov. 17, 1801 AEt. 91

Sacred to the Memory of Violate
by purchase the slave of Amos Fortune
by marriage his wife, by her
fidelity his companion and solace
She died his Widow Sept. 13 1802 AEt. 73

Jaffrey, New Hampshire
1802

AUNT ISRAEL

Here lie Aunt Israel
She dy ob de shakes.
"Bless de Lamb ob God"

Blackville, South Carolina
c. 1850

•

JOHN JAMES COOK

Here lieth
John James Cook
of Newby
Who was a faithful
servant
to his master
and an
Upright downright
honest man.

Ripon, England
1760

•

JACK YORK

Jack York died 1874 age about 85 yrs.
He came to Pittsfield in 1820
Born a Slave in Salem, N.Y.
He was always ready to put his hand out
in friendship to all.

Pittsfield, Vermont
1874

JOHN JACK

God wills us free man wills us slaves.
I will as God wills Gods will be done.

Here lies the body of
JOHN JACK
A native of Africa who died
March 1773 aged about 60 years
Tho' born in a land of slavery,
He was born free,
Tho' he lived in a land of liberty,
He lived a slave,
Till by his honest, tho' stolen labors,
He acquired the source of slavery,
Which gave him his freedom
Tho' not long before,
Death the grand tyrant,
Gave him his final emancipation,
And set him on a footing with kings,
Tho' a slave to vice,
He practised there virtues
Without which kings are but slaves.

Concord, Massachusetts
1773

Short And Sweet

•

Until the cemetery reformation in the second half of the nineteenth century, brevity was never considered a virtue in the composition of epitaphs. Nonetheless, the following certainly get the point across.

•

ASENATH SOULE

> The Chisel can't help her any.

Duxbury, Massachusetts
1865

•

NICHOLAS EVE

> Old & Still

Kittery Point, Maine
c. 1880

RICHARD DENT

> Here lieth Richard Dent
> in his last testement.

Northamptonshire, England
1709

●

HENRY RAPER

> Here Henry Raper
> lies in dust.
> His stature small
> his mind was just.

York, England
1728

●

WILLIAM WIX

> Here lies the body of William Wix
> One thousand, seven hundred and sixty six.

Richmond, England
1766

PHINEAS G. WRIGHT

Going, But Know Not Where.

Putnam, Connecticut
1918

•

THOMAS D'URFEY

TOM · D'URFEY · DIED

Westminster, England
1680

•

JOSEPH PALMER

Persecuted for
Wearing a Beard.

Leonminster, Massachusetts
1873

•

PHILIP HARDING

Received of Philip Harding
his borrowed earth.
July 4th, 1673

Crudwell, England
1673

179

S. B. McCRACKEN

School is Out
Teacher has gone Home

Elkhart, Indiana
1933

●

DR. JOHN GARDNER

DR. JOHN GARDNER'S LAST & BEST BEDROOM

Shoreditch, England
1807

●

SAMUEL CREER

Stop you
Stone Cutters
Here Lays
Sam Creer
1855

Montgomery, Alabama
1855

REVEREND THOMAS MORRIS

MISERIMUS

Worcester, England
1748

●

JONATHAN MOOERS

To die, is but to live forever.

Nantucket, Massachusetts
1815

●

? YORKE

ALAS!
POOR YORKE!

Kent, England
1837

●

MARY RAWSON

Richly embalm'd indeed thou art,
In the Mausoleum of the Heart.

Nantucket, Massachusetts
1851

WILLIAM P. ROTHWELL, M.D.

This is on me.

Pawtucket, Rhode Island
1939

●

LIZZIE JAMES

"I don't know how to die"

East Derry, New Hampshire
1932

●

KING GUSTAVUS III

TANDEM · FELIX
[Happy at last]

Sweden
1792

●

JOHN BURDICK

I Died in a Moment.

Brookville, New York
1823

THOMAS PROCTER

Here lies the body of Thomas Procter
Who lived and died without a doctor.

Luton, England
c. 1800

●

JOHN CUTHBERT

In death no difference is made
Betwixt the sceptre and the spade.

Inverness, Scotland
1711

●

DR. J. J. SUBERS

Been Here
And Gone
Had a Good Time.

Macon, Georgia
1916

PHILLIP SIDNEY

P. S.
The Old Nuisance

East Calais, Vermont
c. 1800

•

LORENZO SABINE

TRANSPLANTED

Eastport, Maine
1877

•

RUTH S. KIBEE

Ruth S. Kibee
The Lord Don't Make Any Mistakes

South Plymouth, New York
1904

SARAH YORKE

> Sarah Yorke this life did resigne
> On May the 13th, '79

Norwich, England
1679

●

ROBERT HALLENBECK FAMILY

> the Family of Robert T. Hallenbeck
> None of us ever voted for
> Roosevelt or Truman

Elgin, Minnesota
c. 1950

●

ADIN N. FRENCH

GONE HOME

Dummerston, Vermont
1855

HENRY DAVID THOREAU

HENRY

Concord, Massachusetts
1862

●

MINETTA STOCKER

In memory of
MINETTA · STOCKER
who quitted this life the fourth of May,
1819, at the age of thirty-nine years.
The smallest woman in this Kingdom
and one of the most accomplished.
She was not more than thirty-three inches high.
She was a native of Austria.

Birmingham, England
1819

Pets

●

Formal burial of man's best friend and other pets has long been big business. The sticky sentiments carved on animal stones could fill a book themselves.

Edwardian epitaph authority E. R. Shuffling called these eulogistic verses "nauseous twaddle," yet he still found one written by his brother about his pet rabbit worthy of note.

●

RECTOR, A DOG

RECTOR
Aged 4 years
Shot
31st March 1890

Ate without stint
Lamb without mint

Llanuwchllyn, North Wales
1890

SIGNOR FIDO, A DOG

To the memory of

SIGNOR FIDO

An Italian of good extraction,

Who came into England,

Not to *bite* us, like most of his countrymen,

But to gain an honest livelihood.

He *hunted* not after fame,

Yet acquired it,

Regardless of the praise of his friends,

But most sensibile of their love.

Tho' he liv'd among the great,

He neither learnt nor flattered any vice.

He was no bigot,

Tho' he doubted of none of the thirty-nine articles:

And if to follow nature,

And to respect the laws of society,

Be philosophy,

He was a perfect philosopher,

A faithful friend,

An agreeable companion,

A loving husband,

And, tho' an Italian,

Was distinguished by a numerous offspring,

All which he liv'd to see take good *courses*.

In his old age he retir'd

To the house of a clergyman in the country,

Where he finish'd his *earthly race*.

And died an honour and an example to the
whole species.

Reader,
This stone is guiltless of flattery;
For he, to whom it was inscrib'd,
Was not a man,
But a GREYHOUND.

Stowe Gardens, England
c. 1880

●

POLLY, A PIG

In
Memory of
POLLY
Mother of
200 Pigs
Died Dec 23rd 1904
Aged 15½ years

Manchester, England
1904

JOHN TWICKENHAM, A RABBIT

Here lies John Twickenham far from where
His eyes first saw the light;
None o'er his grave doth shed a tear,
Now dim those eyes once bright.
He ne'er was known to break his word,
Nor yet deceive a friend;
A lie no mortal ever heard
Escape from his tongue's end.
Perhaps you doubt if mortal man
Attained such faultless habit
But know, my friend, John Twickenham
Was no man,—but a rabbit.

Happisburgh, England
1874

●

BOATSWAIN, LORD BYRON'S DOG (WRITTEN BY BYRON)

Near this spot are deposited the remains of one
Who possessed beauty without vanity,
Strength without insolence,
Courage without ferocity,
And all the virtues of man without his vices.
This praise which would be unmeaning flattery
If inscribed over human ashes
Is but a just tribute to the memory of a dog,
"Boatswain,"
Who was born at Newfoundland May 1803
And died at Newstead Abbey, Nov. 18, 1808

When some proud son of man returns to earth,
Unknown to glory, but upheld by birth,
The sculptor's art exhausts the pomp of woe,
And the storied urns record who rests below;
When all is done upon the tomb is seen,
Not what he was, but what he should have been:
But the poor dog, in life the firmest friend,
The first to welcome, foremost to defend,
Whose honest heart is still his master's own,
Who labours, fights, lives, breathes for him
                    alone,
Unhonoured falls, unnoticed all his worth,
Denied in heaven the soul he held on earth:
While man, vain insect! hopes to be forgiven,
And claims himself a sole exclusive heaven.
Oh! man, thou feeble tenant of an hour,
Debased by slavery or corrupt by power,
Who knows thee well must quit thee with disgust,
Degraded mass of animated dust!
Thy love is lust, thy friendship all a cheat,
Thy smiles hypocrisy, thy words deceit!
By nature vile, ennobled but by name,
Each kindred brute might bid thee blush for
                    shame.
Ye! who perchance behold this simple urn,
Pass on—it honours none you wish to mourn:
To mark a friend's remains these stones arise.
I never knew but one,—& here he lies.

Newstead Abbey, England
1808

ROBIN, A HORSE

Underneath this stone doth lie
Once breathing with sagacity,
The shell of Robin late departed
With all the vigor life imparted.
If a single fault had he,
Let it *forgotten*, *buried* be.

Sark, England
c. 1860

●

FOP, LADY THROCKMORTON'S LAP DOG. (BY WILLIAM COWPER)

Though once a puppy, & though "Fop" by name,
Here moulders one whose bones some honour claim.
No sycophant, although of the Spaniel race,
And, though no hound, a martyr to the chase.
Ye squirrels, rabbits, leverets rejoice!
Your haunts no longer echo to his voice;
This record of his fate, exulting, view,
He died worn out with vain pursuit of you.
"Yes," the indignant shade of Fop replies—
"And, worn with vain pursuit man also dies."

1792

The Famous Go, Too

•

The famous and infamous always had a particular interest in ensuring that posterity recorded the facts as they saw them. To this end, they often composed their own epitaphs as a final statement for history, and each chronicles a particular view of a unique life.

•

BENJAMIN FRANKLIN (BY HIMSELF)

The Body of
B. Franklin
Printer

Like the cover of an old book,
Its contents torn out,
And stripped of its lettering and gilding,
Lies here, Food for worms,
But the work shall not be wholly lost;
For it will, as he believed, Appear once more,
In a new and more perfect Edition
Corrected and Amended
By the Author.

1790

KING THEODORE OF CORSICA

Near this place is interred
THEODORE, King of Corsica,
Who died in this parish December 11th, 1756
Immediately after leaving
the King's Bench Prison,
By benefit of the act of insolvency:
In consequence of which
He registered his kingdom of Corsica
For the use of his creditors.

1756

●

WILLIAM SHAKESPEARE (BY HIMSELF)

Good Friend, for Jesu's sake forbeare
To dig the dust enclosed here.
Blessed be he that spares these stones,
And curst be he that moves my bones.

1616

To the Memory of
Robert Burns, the Ayrshire Bard
who was born at Doonside
On the 29th of January 1759,
and died at Dumfries
On the 22nd of July 1796

O Rabbie Burns, the Man, the Brither,
And art thou goune—and gone for ever;
And has thou crossed that unknown river,
Life's dreary bound?
Like thee, where shall we find anither
The world around?
Go to your sculptur'd tombs, ye Great,
In all the tinsel trash of state;
But by thy honest turf I'll wait,
Thou man of worth.
And weep the sweetest poet's fate,
E'er lived on earth.

1796

MENKAURA — THE THIRD PYRAMID

Osiris, King of the North and South,
Men-Kau-Ra, Living for ever!
The heavens have produced thee
Thou wert engendered by NUT (the sky),
Thou are the offsping of SEB (the earth);
thy mother NUT spreads herself over thee
In her form as a divine mystery.
She has granted thee to be a god.
Thou shalt never more have enemies,
O King of the North and South,
MEN-KAU-RA
Living for ever!

3633 B.C.

●

BRIGHAM YOUNG

Born
on this spot
————1802
A Man of much Courage
and superb
Equipment.

1877

ROBIN HOOD

Here underneath dis laitl stean
Laiz Robert Earl of Huntingdon.
Near arcir ver az hie sae geud,
An pipl kauld im Robin Heud:
Sic an utlawz as hi an is men
Vil England niver si agen.
Obiit 24 Kal, dekembris, 1247

[Here underneath this little stone
Lies Robert, Earl of Huntingdon.
No archer was as he so good,
And people called him Robin Hood.
Such an outlaw as he, and his men,
Will England never see again.]

1247

•

GEORGE FREDERICK HANDEL

To melt the soul, to captivate the ear,
(Angels such melody might deign to hear)
To anticipate on earth the joys of heaven,
'Twas Handel's task: to him that power was given.

1759

KING RICHARD III

I, who am laid beneath this marble stone,
RICHARD the THIRD, possessed the BRITISH THRONE.
My country's guardian in my nephews claim,
By trust betray'd, I to the kingdom came,
Two years and sixty days, save two, I reign'd,
And bravely strove in fight; but unsustain'd
My *English* left me in the luckless field,
Where I to *Henry's* arms was forc'd to yield.
Yet at his cost my corse this tomb obtains,
Who piously interr'd me, and ordains,
That regal honours wait a Kings Remains.
Th' year fourteen hundred was and eighty four,
the twenty-first of *August*, when its power,
And all its rights, I did to the Red Rose restore.
Reader, whoe'er thou art, thy prayers bestow,
T'atone my crimes, and ease my pains below.

1484

●

COPERNICUS

STA · SOL · NE · MOEARE
[Stand, O Sun, move not]

1543

SAMUEL TAYLOR COLERIDGE (BY HIMSELF)

Stop, Christian passer-by; stop, child of God,
And read with gentle breast. Beneath this sod
A poet lies, or that which once seemed he!
O! lift a prayer in thought for S. T. C.!
that he who many a year with toil of breath,
Found death in life—may here find life in death!
Mercy for praise, to be forgiven, for fame!
He asked, and hoped through Christ. Do thou the
same.

1834

•

JESSE JAMES

In Loving Memory of My Beloved Son
Jesse W. James
Died April 13, 1882
Aged 34 Years, 6 Months, 28 Days
Murdered by a Traitor and Coward Whose
Name is not Worthy to Appear Here.

1882

•

ISAAC NEWTON (BY ALEXANDER POPE)

Nature and Nature's Law Lay hid in night;
God said, "Let Newton Be!"—And all was Light.

1727

GEORGE HERMAN "BABE" RUTH (BY CARDINAL SPELLMAN)

> May
> That Divine Spirit
> That Animated
> BABE RUTH
> to Win the Crucial
> Game of Life
> Inspire the Youth
> of America!

1948

●

PLATO

> PLATO's dead form this earthly shroud invests;
> His soul among the godlike heroes rests.

347 B.C.

●

EDGAR ALLAN POE

> "Quoth the Raven Nevermore"

1849

THOMAS PAINE

He lived long, done some good and much harm.

1809

●

ALEXANDER POPE (BY HIMSELF)

For one who would not be buried in Westminster
Abbey.

Heros and Kings your distance keep,
In peace let one poor poet sleep,
Who never flattered folks like you,
Let Horace Blush, and Virgil too.

1744

●

ALEXANDER THE GREAT

SUFFICIT HINC TUMULUS,
CUI NOL SUFFICERET ORBIS

[Here a mound suffices for one for whom the world
was not large enough.]

323 B.C.

JOHN GAY (BY HIMSELF)

Life is a jest & all things show it.
I thought so once, but now I know it.

1732

•

SOPHOCLES

Wind, gentle evergreen, to form a shade
Around the tomb where *Sophocles* is laid.
Sweet ivy, wind thy boughs and intertwine
With blushing roses and the clustering vine.
Thus shall thy lasting leaves, with beauties hung,
Prove grateful emblems of the lays he sung.

406 B.C.

•

ROBERT LOUIS STEVENSON (BY HIMSELF)

Under the wide and starry sky,
Dig the grave and let me lie.
Glad did I live and gladly die,
    And I laid me down with a will.

This be the verse you grave for me:
"Here he lies where he longed to be,
Home is the sailor, home from the sea,
    And the hunter home from the hill."

1894

ROBERT DEVEREAUX, EARL OF ESSEX

Here sleeps great *Essex*, darling of mankind,
Fair Honour's Lamp, four Envy's prey, Art's fame,
Nature's Pride, Vertue's bulwark, lure of the mind,
Wisdom's flower, Valour's tower, Fortune's shame,
  England's sun, *Belgia's* light, *France's* star, *Spain's*
    thunder,
Lisbon's lightning, *Ireland's* cloud, the whole world's
    wonder.

beheaded, 1601

●

SIR WALTER RALEIGH (BY HIMSELF)

Even such is time, which takes in trust
Our youth and joyes, and all we have,
And payes us but with age and dust,
Which in the darke and silent grave
When wee have wandered all our wayes,
Shuts up the story of our dayes:
And from which earth, and grave, and dust,
The Lord shall rise me up, I trust.

beheaded, 1618

EDWARD THE BLACK PRINCE

Whoe'er thou art with lips comprest
That passest where this corpse doth rest,
To that I tell thee, list, O man!
So far as I tell thee can,
Such as thou art, I was but now
And as I am so shalt be thou;
Death little did my thoughts employ,
So long as life I did enjoy
On earth great riches were my fate,
With which I kept a noble state;
Great lands, great houses, treasures great,
Hanging and horses, gold and plate.
But now I am but poor and base,
Deep in the earth is now my place;
My flesh is wasted all away,
Reduced my splendour to decay;
My house is very straight and short,
Forsooth to me is utter naught:
Nay such a change has passed o'er me,
That, could you now my features see,
I scarcely think you aught could scan
To show that I was once a man.
For God's sake pray the heavenly king
That he my soul to mercy bring!
All who for me their prayers shall spend
Or me to God shall recommend,
God make his paradise their home,
Wherein no wicked soul may come.

1376

Suggested Reading

•

Anderson, M. L. *Looking for History in British Churches*. London: John Murray, 1951.

Andrew, William. *Curious Epitaphs*. London: William Andrew, 1899. (Available through antiquarian booksellers.)

Aries, Philippe. *The Hour of Our Death*. New York: Knopf, 1981.

Beable, W. H. *Epitaphs, Graveyard Humor & Eulogy*. New York: Thomas Y. Crowell Company, 1925. (Available through antiquarian booksellers.)

Bland, Olivia. *The Royal Way of Death*. London: Constable and Company, 1986.

Brown, Raymond. *A Book of Epitaphs*. New York: Taplinger, 1969.

Cansick, Frederick Teague. *Epitaphs of Middlesex*. London: 1875. (Available through antiquarian booksellers.)

Coffin, Margaret. *Death in Early America*. New York: Elsevier/Nelson Books, 1976.

Duval, Francis Y., and Ivan B. Rigby. *Early American Gravestone Art in Photographs*. New York: Dover, 1978.

Enright, D. J., ed. *The Oxford Book of Death*. Oxford, England: Oxford University Press, 1983.

Fowle, John A. *Old Dorchester Burying Ground 1634*. Dorchester, Mass.: Society of "Ye Old Blake House," 1907. (Available through antiquarian booksellers.)

George, Diana Hume, and Malcolm A. Nelson. *Epitaph & Icon: A Field Guide to the Old Burying Grounds of Cape Cod, Martha's Vineyard & Nantucket*. Orleans, Mass.: Parnassus Imprints, 1983.

Gillion, E. V. *Early New England Gravestone Rubbings*. New York: Dover, 1966.

Howe, W. H. *Here Lies*. New York: New Amsterdam Book Company, 1902. (Available through antiquarian booksellers.)

Huber, Leonard V., Peggy McDowell, and Mary Louise Christovich. *New Orleans Architecture*. Vol. 3, *The Cemeteries*. Gretna, La.: Pelican Publishing Company, 1974.

Jacobs, C. Walker. *Stranger Stop and Cast an Eye*. Brattleboro, Vt.: Stephen Greene Press, 1972.

Jones, Barbara. *Design for Death*. Indianapolis, Ind.: Bobbs-Merrill, 1967.

Kippax, John R. *Churchyard Literature*. Reprinted from 1876 volume. Williamstown, Mass.: Corner House Publishers, 1978.

Le Neve, John. *Monumenta Anglicana*. London, 1719. (Available on microfilm in large research libraries, or antiquarian booksellers in England.)

Mann, Thomas C., and Janet Greene. *Over Their Dead Bodies: Yankee Epitaphs & History*. Brattleboro, Vt.: Stephen Greene Press, 1962.

Morley, John. *Death, Heaven and the Victorians*. Pittsburgh, Pa.: University of Pittsburgh Press, 1971.

Pettigrew, Thomas Joseph. *Chronicles of the Tombs*. Lon-

don: Bell & Daldy, 1857. (Available through antiquarian booksellers.)

————. *The Sexton's Monitor and Dorchester Cemetery Me-
morial*. Boston: Alfred Mudge, 1838. (Available
through antiquarian booksellers.)

Spiegl, Fritz, ed. *A Small Book of Grave Humour*. London:
Pan Books, Ltd., 1971.

————. *Dead Funny: Another Book of Grave Humour*. London: Pan Books, Ltd., 1982.

Suffling, Ernest R. *Epitaphia*. London: L. Upcott Gill,
1909. (Available through antiquarian booksellers in
England.)

Wallis, Charles W. *American Epitaphs, Grave and Humorous*. New York: Dover, 1973.

Weever, John. *Ancient Funeral Monuments*. London, 1631.
(Available on microfilm in large research libraries.)

Whitmore, William H. *The Graveyards of Boston*. Albany,
N.Y.: Joel Munsell, 1878. (Available through antiquarian booksellers.)

E. R. SHUSHAN

Stop here my friends and cast an eye,
You should all read this book before you die.
I've travelled the world, from burial ground to
mortuary,
In hopes of finding the perfect cemetery.
After years of research, I must make a confession:
I've finally turned grave robbing into an honest
profession.

New York City
Oct. 31, 1990